THE PRUDENT INVESTOR'S GUIDE TO BEATING THE MARKET

John J. Bowen, Jr.
Carl H. Reinhardt
Alan B. Werba

IRWIN
Professional Publishing®
Chicago • London • Singapore

 **IRWIN   Concerned about Our Environment**

In recognition of the fact that our company is a large end-user of fragile yet replenishable resources, we at IRWIN can assure you that every effort is made to meet or exceed Environmental Protection Agency (EPA) recommendations and requirements for a "greener" workplace.

To preserve these natural assets, a number of environmental policies, both companywide and department-specific, have been implemented. From the use of 50% recycled paper in our textbooks to the printing of promotional materials with recycled stock and soy inks to our office paper recycling program, we are committed to reducing waste and replacing environmentally unsafe products with safer alternatives.

© Richard D. Irwin, a Times Mirror Higher Education Group, Inc. company, 1996

All rights reserved. No part of this publication may be reproduced, stored in a retrieval system, or transmitted, in any form or by any means, electronic, mechanical, photocopying, recording, or otherwise, without the prior written permission of the publisher.

This publication is designed to provide accurate and authoritative information in regard to the subject matter covered. It is sold with the understanding that neither the author or the publisher is engaged in rendering legal, accounting, or other professional service. If legal advice or other expert assistance is required, the services of a competent professional person should be sought.

From a Declaration of Principles jointly adopted by a Committee of the American Bar Association and a Committee of Publishers.

Irwin Professional Book Team

Publisher: Wayne McGuirt
Executive editor: Amy Hollands Gaber
Production supervisor: Pat Frederickson
Assistant manager, desktop services: Jon Christopher
Project editor: Paula M. Buschman
Senior designer: Larry J. Cope
Art studio: Bensen Studios, Inc.
Compositor: Bensen Studios, Inc.
Typeface: 11/13 Times Roman
Printer: Buxton Skinner Printing Co.

**Times Mirror
Higher Education Group**

Library of Congress Cataloging-in-Publication Data

The prudent investor's guide to beating the market / John J. Bowen, Jr.; Carl H. Reinhardt; Alan B. Werba ; Larry Chambers, [editor].
   p. cm.
   Includes index.
   ISBN 0-7863-0365-4
   1. Investments—Handbooks, manuals, etc. I. Chambers, Larry,
II. Reinhardt Werba Bowen Advisory Services.
HG4527.P78 1996
332.6—dc20   95–22723

Printed in the United States of America
1 2 3 4 5 6 7 8 9 0 BS 2 1 0 9 8 7 6

Foreword

I am extremely pleased to write the foreword for this book as it represents the articulation of the views and the investment philosophy which I myself believe and follow with my own clients. The truly astounding aspect of these investment concepts is that they represent the clearest understanding of how the world of stock and bond investing truly works—not how we think it works, not through some "new" or "secret" discovery which the authors have made; but rather, how stocks and bonds actually function within a free-market economic system.

This book, and the concepts it represents, is an outgrowth of an evolution in thought regarding the prudent management of risk and the capture of consistent long-term growth by investing strategically with asset class mutual funds. It is about taking advantage of the most current thinking which is available today, and designing portfolios which use this knowledge successfully. It is about stepping into the world of rational thought and empirical evidence; and out of the world of emotional "feelings" and commission-driven "advice."

The investment arena is in the middle of a quantum leap forward in our ability to design portfolios which efficiently account for the risks associated with stock and bond investing. The tools and methodologies available to us have evolved dramatically within just the last four or five years. The authors of this book have successfully presented this knowledge in a manner which is easily understood and useable for the average investor who is serious about asset growth.

What this book does so well is to introduce some of the most exciting investment concepts to come along since Harry Markowitz pioneered the development of Modern Portfolio Theory during the 1950s. Having been intimately involved with the evolution of this thinking, I want to share the story with you of how I personally became involved with both the precepts of this book, and with its co-author. I want to explain just why it is critically important for the serious investor to read this book from cover to cover. It is the financial survival guide for your assets.

For over a decade, I provided fee-based consulting and investment advisory services to small-to-medium sized institutional investors. These were traditional consulting services involving investment definition, policy design, asset allocation, management searches, and performance/attribution analysis. One of the most important of these services was the quarterly performance and attribution evaluations in which the performance of a portfolio was dissected in order to provide an understanding of "where the returns came from," and who should get the credit—the money manager or the market.

From these analyses my clients and I would make long-term decisions regarding how best (and who best) to manage their money. We would attempt to target and blend complementary investment "styles" in order to "smooth out" the overall volatility. We would have, at a minimum, both "value" and "growth" styles, since these approaches tended to be contrary to one another, and tended to move counter-cyclically in their ability to produce positive returns.

Our goal was to always "add value." Adding value meant providing additional performance over time after subtracting out the performance of the market, risk-free investments like Treasury bills, management fees, and transaction costs. During my first ten years of doing this, I noticed money managers would add value over short periods of time; then, lose that value as the time periods were extended. Long-term consistency was a major problem.

Beginning around 1990, the stock market became increasingly flat and performance from my clients' managers seemed to be harder to come by (especially on a "value-added" basis). My analyses of individual managers, both those being used by clients, as well as within institutional databases, demonstrated increased levels of inconsistency. When plotted on a Risk vs. Return graph, their positions on that graph were seldom the same from one quarter to another. Control of volatility relative to the market seemed unavailable to most managers.

It become abundantly clear that there was simply no value being added by the traditional active management approach. In fact, in most instances, regardless of style, when performance horizons exceeded a five to ten year time period, value was actually being lost. The only managers who even remotely came close to adding value of any sort, and then only in a very incremental fashion, were those who classified themselves as Asset Allocators. But even the Allocators experienced value-added measurements of zero, when the time horizons were stretched out seven to ten years. Virtually all performance could be attributed to the market.

This realization combined with a decade's worth of experience created a professional and intellectual dilemma. In order for me to continue to provide legitimate advice to clients based upon legitimate analysis, I had to understand why this was occurring, and what actions we must take to achieve our long-term goals. So began my search which led me to an in-depth study of what had been and was being proven academically and empirically. I read everything I could find on the subject as part of my due diligence, and in a very short time the answers became overwhelmingly obvious. The indisputable facts combined with new academic work provided absolute validation of what my clients and I were experiencing in the real world.

My research efforts literally caused an intellectual metamorphosis which I can honestly describe was the closest thing to a professional religious experience. My conclusions shook the very foundation of my beliefs about how markets work, and subsequently how to invest within them. After a decade of providing high level investment advice, it was obvious: "Traditional active money management does not work!"

By "work" I mean it doesn't add value. Traditional management's long-term results merely come from what the market provides, and is no better than that which can be obtained from random chance, like that seen when flipping a coin, or throwing darts at a stock table.

My primary function as a fee-based advisor was to provide the best possible advice based upon the best knowledge that I could obtain. My research, combined with my professional experience, opened my eyes to the only true method of investing for the serious investor. This, in turn, leads me back to this book and why I am writing this foreword.

The co-author of this book, John Bowen, and I came upon each other by happenstance. After concluding the above, I began to study methods of how to "immunize" portfolios against loss by using "index-type" mutual funds, or those which provided performance and volatility that were close to specific unmanaged indexes. An office colleague brought to my attention an article in a magazine which discussed the very concepts and conclusions which I had arrived at a short time before. (This colleague, along with others had endured my ranting about my conclusions and therefore, thought I might enjoy knowing I was not alone in my beliefs.) Within this article, a gentleman named John Bowen was discussing the identical conclusions and concepts. This prompted me to pick up the phone and make contact with John. After some discussions, we agreed it would make sense for us to meet and share our collective thoughts and methodologies.

The rest, as the cliché goes, is history. Since that time I have worked with John and his company providing the investment advisory services to clients which acknowledge and take advantage of the empirically proven techniques discussed so well within this book. In fact, our views are so closely aligned that John and I are currently co-authoring another book which will bring the concepts and conclusions of Strategically Designed Asset Class Portfolios to the small to medium institutionally-sized investor.

It is within this environment that I have so willingly written this foreword. Read, study, and apply the information this book discusses to your own investments. Whether you are an institutional investor, or an individual with a serious mindset about the future of your own money, the use of strategically managed portfolios using asset class mutual funds is the only rational, intelligent approach to obtaining consistent long-term results.

Let me leave you with one last thought. Investing and portfolio design is not static with a complete understanding of all knowledge. Think of it in the same way you think of the field of medicine. Fifty or a hundred years ago, physicians followed methodologies and applied techniques that today would be considered malpractice, costing them perhaps millions of dollars in damages in litigation. But at the time, their actions were based upon the best information they had, along with the best understanding of how the human body functions. What's changed is an expansion of knowledge and understanding based upon scientific, empirical study that has produced a "better" way.

The field of investing and portfolio design has done the same thing. Ten or fifteen years ago, our understanding of risk and how to manage it presented us with a set of choices which were "the best" at the time. Like the analogy of the doctor, the investor now have new, more current information with which to make successful investment choices. This information is in your hands right now. Read it and enjoy. Your investment life will never be the same.

John W. Byrd, President and CEO
Byrd Capital Market Advisers, Inc.
Arlington, Texas, (800) 707-2262

Acknowledgments

This book will help prudent investors beat the market by applying the frontier of investment knowledge. This is not a textbook; it's an academic-based roadmap, clearly illustrating how you can implement the same investment strategies that were once only available to billion-dollar pension plans.

We would like to begin by thanking three leading members of the financial economic community: Harry Markowitz, Merton Miller, and William Sharpe, whose research was awarded the Nobel prize in economics and provides the foundation for this book. In addition, we would like to thank Eugene Fama, Ken French, and Meir Statman for their academic research and guidance.

No one deserves more credit for the application of this research than the principals of Dimensional Fund Advisors, Rex Sinquefield and David Booth. They were early pioneers in developing and applying investment strategies for the institutional investor. They joined with us to bring these same strategies to private clients. Dan Wheeler, one of the directors of Dimensional, made this effort possible and successful. We would also like to thank Gene Fama, Jr., Art Barlow, David Plecha and Jeanne Sinquefield for their continuous guidance in the application of these investment theories.

One of the missing links to the implementation of these strategies was the creation of a mutual fund marketplace. Charles Schwab & Co. made this possible. We would like to thank Charles Schwab, John Coghlan, Dennis Clark, Nick Georgis, and Jim Hackley for their contributions.

We are deeply grateful to our publisher, Irwin Professional Publishing, who saw the value that individual readers would receive from this book and gave us the opportunity to do it, and to our editor Amy Gaber for her patience, editorial guidance, and encouragement.

To make this a reality we needed an alter ego. We want to thank Larry Chambers of Chambers & Associates, our writing coach. Any professional writing a book would be fortunate to have such an outstanding guide and sounding board.

This book would not have been possible without the independent financial advisors who chose to work with us in bringing these strategies to individual investors. We would particularly like to thank Harold Anderson, Jeff Berg, Tim Bock, Ken Boone, Joe Bowie, Gene Burns, John Burroughs, John Byrd, Eileen Clune, Mel Cooper, John Deaton, Max DeZemlen, Linda DeZemplen, Mike Dixon, Bob Ericson, Maurice Glazer, Dan Goldie, Tony Hannon, Michael Irving, Russ Ketron, Bob Kresek, Greg Lucas, Craig Martin, Carl Mehl, Robert Newell, Paul Pennington, Gary Pia, Richard Robb, Mark Sievers, Harry Tyler, Arvin Vaughan, Floyd Walling and Michael Weakley.

Thanks to the staff of Reinhardt Werba Bowen Advisory Services for their tireless efforts in making this book happen; Mark Mushet, for his diligent review of all the data and graphs; Pat Goyeau, for the illustrations she created; Jan Garred, who assists us through each revision; Marlene Bass, for maintaining our schedules; and Betty Kabanek, Sandra Baseman, Warren Herr, Stan Carson, Dave Richardson, Guy Ridout, Ben Bingaman, Rich Boone, Scott Leonard, and Alex Potts for their insights into refining our message; to Bonnie Boone and Nicole Fowler, for their help in distribution; to our board members, Ken Koskella, Chuck Masters, and Joe Shepela, for their wisdom.

Thank you to our special good friends, Steve Moeller with StTR; Jeff Saccacio, Steve Gissiner, Keith Clark, Eddie Kimura, Phil Croy, and John Grady with Coopers & Lybrand; Regina Saborsky with Mitchell, Silberberg & Knupp; Bill Bachrach; Mario Capozzoli with the American Cancer Society; Jim Jorgensen with "It's Your Money"; The International Association for Financial Planning; and The Institute for Investment Management Consultants for their assistance.

Most of all we want to sincerely thank our thousands of clients who have entrusted us with their life savings. They placed their confidence in us and allowed us to pioneer these strategies for private clients.

Contents

Chapter One

Introduction

I f we could show you how to prudently and consistently "beat the stock market" at a low cost, would you be willing to spend a day learning how? After reading this book, you will not only know how to invest confidently, you will no longer feel the need to search every financial publication for the latest investment insights.

My name is John Bowen. I am the chief executive officer (CEO) and president of Reinhardt Werba Bowen Advisory Services, an independent investment advisory firm located in California's Silicon Valley. Our clients tell us our approach has been a liberating and profitable experience. We believe you will feel the same way.

At first glance, this book may look like every other book on investing. You may have even heard these same promises before. That's OK. We invite you to be skeptical; in fact, that attitude is the best tool you have for investing. Nevertheless, investing can be easy and understandable—that's why we've written this book.

In the 1980s, dramatic changes affected our investment community. The quantity of investment products available to the public increased exponentially, while the quality diminished significantly. These were very frustrating times for us.

As a successful financial planning firm working with thousands of individual clients, we helped our clients reach their financial goals. As part of this process, we prepared for our clients an elaborate financial plan that clearly lays out the path to the successful attainment of their financial goals, including investment recommendations. If the outside investments we relied on to implement these strategies performed to their stated expectations, our clients would achieve their financial goals. However, in many cases the results of these investments were disappointing at best in the 1980s. You may have had similar experiences with some of your own investments. What good were the financial plans our clients had if the underlying investments were not doing what was expected?

This frustration caused our firm to begin a search for a better solution. At the time, I was teaching investment theory in the MBA (master in business administration) program at Golden Gate University in San Francisco. I was teaching the successful investment strategies of institutional investors. It bore little resemblance to the methods used by individual investors. Most of the advice available to individual investors had little to do with the principles of investment theory, and much of it just did not make economic sense. We knew there must be a better strategy for implementing investments than what most of Wall Street was touting, but it wasn't clear to us how to apply it. We spent the next five years looking for answers.

Our quest led us to the top academics in the field of financial economics. They had the answers for how to beat the market. What they were saying was backed up by a mountain of research and proof, but only the very largest institutions were taking advantage of this knowledge. The concepts they developed won the Nobel Prize in Economics in 1990 and are known collectively as Modern Portfolio Theory.

We realized if we could discover a way for the individual investor to have the same advantage as institutions, our clients would gain a tremendous added benefit from our services. They certainly would beat the market averages, and they would be on the road to fulfilling their financial goals.

At first we weren't sure that investors would understand the concepts. Many in the academic community attempted to discourage us from communicating these concepts to our clients. They were used to dealing with their fellow academics or with the investment committees of large pension plans. They felt these strategies would be too complicated for the private investor and would confuse them to inaction. But we discovered that the logic is so compelling our clients were quick to grasp it.

When our clients invest their life savings, they are more than willing to spend some time to understand how investments really work. Amazingly, these new strategies actually simplified the investment decision-making process and made our clients feel free to focus on other parts of their lives.

Once it was clear that our clients were understanding them, we wanted to communicate these strategies to as many people as possible. If investors truly understood how markets work, they would be able to participate.

Using the techniques we call Asset Class Investing, they could secure their financial futures for their families. An asset class is a group of securities with the same risk characteristics, such as an index mutual fund. Asset Class Investing is the way we describe the process of building portfolios utilizing index and enhanced-index mutual funds. An index fund is a mutual fund that attempts to replicate a financial market index such as Standard & Poor's 500. The S&P 500 is made up of 500 large, public companies. An enhanced-index mutual fund attempts to add value through a greater understanding of how financial markets work.

The communication of these strategies became the new mission of our firm and the reason we undertook the writing of this book. We wanted to show investors how they could, by being prudent, actually beat the market. Unfortunately, it is not a get-rich-quick strategy, but one that will take patience. The payoff to your family can be significant, if properly implemented.

WHO SHOULD READ THIS BOOK?

We believe there are basically three different types of investors: (1) conservative, (2) aggressive, and (3) prudent. People in the first group think the stock and bond markets are really casinos. To protect their principal, these people invest primarily in certificates of deposit (CDs) and money market funds. These types of investments offer stability of principal. But with CD rates usually just keeping up with inflation, these investors are looking for higher returns—without going out on a limb. They know they are often setting themselves up for failure in reaching their goals with the low rates of return, but they are uncomfortable making any changes until they are sure they are doing the right thing. They want to know what their options are. We will illustrate how the conservative investors can fulfill their desire for low risk while satisfying their need for growth.

The second type of investor wants aggressive growth. People in this group usually have a brokerage account and call their own shots—often with the help of stockbrokers. These investors would like to earn double-digit returns. But it seems they are always late in finding the next hot investment or "investment guru." If these investors make the wrong decisions, they'll get hammered; they'll be worse off than when they started. They intuitively know there must be a better way, but they are just not sure what it is. However, they are going to keep trying until they find it. Using our strategies, they will have a higher likelihood of achieving their goals consistently over time, with substantially lower risk.

The third group of investors is the largest. These people fit some-where in between the first two extremes. They're basically conservative and safety conscious, but they want to earn a fair return on their invest-ments. We call these people prudent investors. These are the ones who will benefit the most from this book.

Prudent investors are willing to take some risk—if the returns are commensurate. They are often uncomfortable with investments because they do not understand how investments work. It's not that they are not smart enough; it's just that they have not been exposed to these con-cepts. Often they work with investment advisors, many of whom ask their clients to have faith that they know what they are doing and that their actions are in the client's best interests. They say, "Trust me." Unfortunately, you already know the all-too-frequent result. In this book, we are not going to ask you to take a leap of faith. This book will empower you to make the correct decisions for yourself or, if you wish, to choose an advisor who can implement its principles.

There is an intelligent approach that will work for all investors in meet-ing their personal financial goals. It starts by freeing your mind of all the self-serving investment advice you have received in the past and learning how investments work. We believe the solution is to capitalize on a series of world-renowned investment strategies developed primarily at the University of Chicago.

THE BEGINNING OF ASSET CLASS INVESTING

It all started in March 1952, when arguably the most famous insight in the history of modern investing was published. It appeared in the *Journal of Finance*; its author was a then-unknown 25-year-old graduate student named Harry Markowitz.[1] Markowitz is credited with forging a new way of looking at how we divide our assets so we can minimize risk and maximize returns.

For years, Markowitz had been wrestling with a broad philosophical question: How can people make the best possible decisions when deal-ing with the inescapable trade-offs in life? He knew that investors faced especially tough questions. How can you earn attractive returns without accepting undue amounts of risk? How much risk is necessary to achieve your goals?

Using mathematics to solve this puzzle, Markowitz discovered a remark-able new way to build an investment portfolio. He was guided by one assumption: He believed that it was possible to minimize risks and improve returns scientifically in a diversified portfolio.

He eventually developed a scientifically balanced portfolio. Based upon his study of historical investment performance, he created the best combination of different securities. Markowitz called this "mathematically correct" portfolio an *efficient portfolio*. His method seeks to achieve maximum returns with the least amount of risk. The scientific system that Markowitz pioneered eventually became known as Modern Portfolio Theory.

These powerful investment strategies work equally well for conservative, prudent, or aggressive investors. You can use the investment strategies based on Modern Portfolio Theory to build your own portfolio for retirement, to protect your assets once you've retired, or to meet other financial goals. These strategies are universal in their application.

Amazingly, these strategies actually simplify the investment decision-making process. You'll learn how to maximize your expected returns while simplifying your investment decisions. You can use these investment strategies to protect your principal, generate income growth, or maximize expected portfolio growth.

Markowitz first published the theoretical foundation for Modern Portfolio Theory over 40 years ago. Since then, his ideas have been tested and refined. These strategies are now accepted worldwide as an authoritative "blueprint" for prudent investing—that is, "wisely and cautiously providing for the future."

RETHINK ALL INVESTMENT ADVICE

One well-known study that examined many concepts of Modern Portfolio Theory will make you rethink the investment advice you've been getting. In 1986, a prestigious pension-fund consulting firm released a startling research report. The firm analyzed the performance variations of 91 large pension funds.[2] The conclusions sent shock waves through the traditional investment management community.

The report analyzed the three primary investment strategies that determine variations in portfolio performance: market timing, stock selection, and asset allocation.

Here's what should concern you: The two strategies that had the least impact on performance were market timing and securities selection.

Most investors spend all of their time on what was determined to be least important. On average, these two strategies did not add value; in fact, they lost value.

Both of these strategies rely on attempts to predict the future. Most stockbrokers' recommendations to individual investors are based on these two strategies. Wall Street firms spend billions of dollars each year trying to outguess their competition in these two areas. The management strategy that had the most positive impact on portfolio performance is not yet widely recommended for individual investors. But this third strategy, asset allocation, accounted for over 90 percent of the profit determination. This powerful concept is the foundation for Modern Portfolio Theory. It's a simple but little-used technique that anyone can apply.

WHY ISN'T EVERYONE USING THESE STRATEGIES?

If Modern Portfolio Theory is so popular now with institutional investors, why aren't individual investors using it? We have often wondered about this ourselves, especially since it's now taught in basic finance classes at most of the major universities.

We suspect that there's one main reason why the majority of the public doesn't know about Modern Portfolio Theory: Most major brokerage firms aren't in the business of educating the investing public. Their primary concern is their own profits. Many stockbrokers are taught to drive transactions by pushing their clients' emotional hot buttons. Most make their money on commissions, not performance. A well-informed public could dramatically cut into those brokers' profits.

Even the most senior members of the investment community began to question why, given the long success of Modern Portfolio Theory, it had not met widespread acceptance.[3] The organizational politics of the major financial services firms made this acceptance almost impossible.

What about the media? Aren't magazines and TV shows in business to help investors make informed decisions? No. They're in business to make money for their owners and advertisers. The media thrives on volatility and uncertainty. If everyone knew how to invest scientifically, there wouldn't be a need for media gurus. Sales of magazines and newsletters would plummet. Profits would suffer. Other people's self-interest is the main reason that more individual investors aren't using Modern Portfolio Theory.

WHY DID WE WRITE THIS BOOK?

At our firm, Reinhardt Werba Bowen Advisory Services, we have a different philosophy. It's very simple. We believe in sharing our knowledge of investments with everyone who's interested. We also believe that informed investors are our best clients. That's why our firm decided to write this book. We believe there are many intelligent investors who would work with us if they understood how the markets worked and how our strategies can easily be implemented. So we wrote this book out of our enlightened self-interest. We know we can achieve our goals if we help enough investors achieve theirs.

Our strategies will de-mystify the investment management process. You will gain more control over your long-term investment returns—without the need to predict interest rate movements or stock market directions. Our methodologies enable you to build a scientific portfolio of stocks, bonds, and cash that will allow you to beat the market.

You'll quickly understand why these practical ideas set the standards for prudent investing all over the world. We will start by explaining the five fundamental needs that all successful investors must meet. Most people do not have a plan to address each of their needs. But ignoring them won't make them go away. We will illustrate clearly how you can safely and prudently reach all of your investment objectives, while overcoming the common frustrations most investors face.

You'll learn how professionals identify and quantify investment risks. You will clearly see the historical risk/reward relationship between different types of investments and why some investments have consistently outperformed others. And you will also discover the professional's secret for taming market volatility.

Next, you'll learn how to use the five principles of Asset Class Investing to scientifically balance your investment portfolio. These techniques will enable you to design portfolios with the specific levels of risk that meet your individual comfort level while maximizing your return. We'll explain how to counterbalance different investment classes to maximize your expected returns. This easy-to-use investment strategy has historically and consistently beaten those of professional managers.

Then you will uncover the hidden costs of investing in mutual funds. Most no-load mutual funds chronically underperform against industry or market benchmarks. We will show you how, like institutional investors, you can slash your administrative and transaction costs up to 75 percent.

In the last chapters of the book, you will learn how to match your risk comfort level to a scientifically designed model portfolio. These portfolios use the most cost-effective building blocks available to create an efficient portfolio. In this section, you'll see your different investment options and the most likely outcomes of each. You'll learn what you can realistically expect to earn from the investment portfolio you construct.

By the time you have read the first two chapters, you'll understand why more than one-third of the major pension plans are using these same methods. This is not a textbook; it is not written for the academic community. It is written as a guide for the prudent investor. We have tried to have fun in communicating this information and have taken some very technical subjects and attempted to make them understandable. Leave all your thoughts and preconceptions about investing behind and walk with us through this process.

It is not critical that you understand everything we have written in this book. In fact, most individuals will still want to work with an investment advisor. That's fine. What you need to know is whether the advisor understands these concepts and can implement them on your behalf. In Chapter Fourteen, we will outline the questions you should ask in selecting your investment advisor. This will give you the confidence to move forward, either with an advisor or on your own.

ENDNOTES

[1]Markowitz, Harry, *The Journal of Finance* 7, no. 1 (March 1952), pp. 77-91.

[2]Brinson, Gary P.; L. Randolph Hood; and Gilbert L. Beebower, *Financial Analysts Journal*, July-August 1986, pp. 39-44.

[3]Michaud, Richard, *Financial Analysts Journal*, January-February 1989, pp. 31-42.

Chapter Two

Five Key Concepts of Investment Success

In working with thousands of investors in all walks of life, from individuals just getting started to the CEOs of some of the largest corporations in the country, we have identified several fundamental needs facing all of them. In this chapter, we will begin by identifying the five fundamental needs that all investors have. Next, we will show you how we have successfully met those needs through our five key concepts to investment success. Following these five concepts will allow you to meet your financial needs.

RISK AVERSION

Investors are risk averse. Some might argue that a better phrase might be "risk ignorant." Only a few investors truly understand the concept of risk. If they did, the number of investors who have been disappointed in how their investments have worked would be cut in half. Most investors do not know the risks they are taking and often take inappropriate risks, which results in a huge number of lawsuits and arbitration hearings. Billions of dollars are still sitting in bank savings accounts, which yield approximately the inflation rate, due to this aversion to risk.

Most investors recognize that they are taking some risk, but do not know how to quantify the amount. Even U.S. Treasury bills, which are often referred to as a risk-free investment, are not risk free. When you calculate their net return after taxes and inflation, you are often assured of little or no return at all. Prudent investors want to know how best to safeguard their life savings. By understanding the risk/return trade-offs and embracing the level of risk with which you feel comfortable, you can not only control risk, but also maximize your return.

FIGURE 2–1

S&P 500 Total Return: Normal Distribution

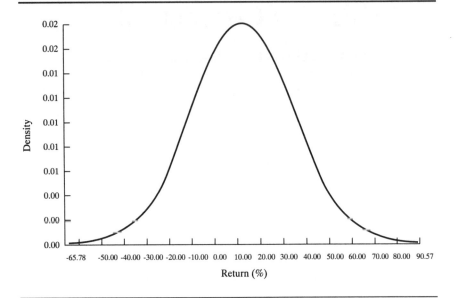

Source: Ibbotson and Associates.

A key component of any investment plan is understanding and measuring risk. What is risk? Risk is nothing more than the uncertainty of future rates of return. Risk is created by the volatility of the marketplace. Volatility measures the rate and range of up and down movements in the price of a security. Will Rogers used to say, "Don't tell me about the return on my money until you tell me about the return of my money." The less certain you are that an investment's actual return will be close to its expected return, the more risk that investment carries.

The historical risk of an investment can be statistically measured using the standard deviation to signify volatility in terms of past performance. Standard deviations describe how far from the mean (average), either higher or lower, the performance has been. If the distribution of returns is normal, one standard deviation added to or subtracted from the mean will encompass about 68 percent of the occurrences; two standard deviations cover approximately 95 percent. For example, in Figure 2–1, the average arithmetic annual return from 1926 to 1994 for the S&P 500 was 12.2 percent. The standard deviation for the S&P 500 for that period was 20.3.

FIGURE 2–2

Annual Distributions of S&P 500 Returns 1926–94

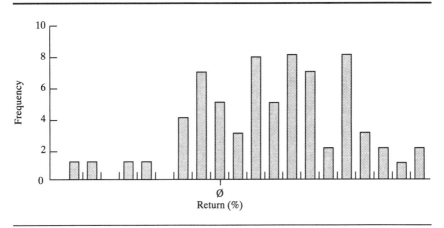

Source: Roger G. Ibbotson and Rex A. Sinquefield, *Stocks, Bonds, Bills and Inflation.*

We would expect that returns would fall between -8.1 percent and 32.5 percent approximately two thirds (68 percent) of the time, if we utilize the S&P 500 index's historical standard deviation of 20.3. The higher the standard deviation of return, the higher the risk involved in the investment.

In Figure 2-1, we have illustrated what the distribution of returns would have been if they occurred as a normal, bell-shaped distribution. Figure 2-2 illustrates the frequency of distributions for the S&P 500 index from 1926 to 1994.

While the latter distribution is not perfectly normal, the standard-deviation measure helps explain what the distribution is likely to be. The greater the range of returns—the greater the risk—the larger the standard deviation.

Generally, the current price of a security reflects both the expected total return on an investment and its perceived risk. The lower the risk, the lower the return. Risks can be classified in two broad categories: loss of principal and loss of purchasing power. The risk of losing principal comes from investing in securities whose values fluctuate due to either systematic or nonsystematic risk. Systematic or nondiversifiable risk is common to the whole economy and cannot be diversified away. A measure of extra return, or a risk premium, is demanded by investors to bear this market risk.

Nonsystematic or diversifiable risks are those associated with individual companies and are independent of market risk. Nonsystematic risk can be easily diversified away. The market does not reward you for risks that can be diversified away. The risk of losing purchasing power is generally derived from investing in assets whose expected rates of return are too low to counter the erosion of their principal value by taxes and inflation.

Each investor has his or her own risk-tolerance level. This level reflects the risk you are willing to take to receive a specified, expected rate of return and your financial condition, objectives, and needs. You should not take more risk than you are comfortable with; doing so is the surest road to financial failure. If there is a downturn and you have taken more risk than you are comfortable with, you will close your investment account and probably promise yourself that you will never do that again. If you designed your portfolio with your risk tolerance in mind, when the downturn comes, you will be able to ride it out to investment success. In Chapter Eight, we will show you how to calculate your own risk-tolerance level.

RETURN ENHANCEMENT

If you are like most investors, you want the greatest total return possible. This is the essence of the selection process most investors go through when they read the financial press and consult their stockbrokers or financial advisors. They are looking for the best way to enhance their returns within the framework of some acceptable level of risk.

It is easy to believe that there is an investment guru out there who can point out the investments that have high expected rates of return with little or, better yet, no risk. If only we search a little harder, we can find the right oracle. The media plays to this pursuit. Most investors do not think of themselves as sufficiently knowledgeable, so they are tempted to grasp at the newest prophecy by the latest superstar investment guru. Our society reinforces hero worship.

Success in this search for the investment Holy Grail is not found through an active manager who will "show you the light," but in achieving an understanding of how markets work. You need to become sophisticated in the underlying concepts of investing instead of focusing on the last few years of a mutual fund's performance.

Our definition of a sophisticated investor is anyone who has invested money at least once, lost it, and didn't like the empty feeling they were left with. Most investors certainly meet that definition. Think of your own investment experiences. The challenge every sophisticated investor faces in the quest for return enhancement is to resist getting caught up in the numerous investment magazines and newsletters that play to our emotions and offer contradictory advice. One of the reasons why many investors fail is because decisions are often based on misleading information.

Most investors are noise investors. They believe that by reading *The Wall Street Journal* each morning, they have become insiders. Noise investors think they are trading on information that gives them some advantage. Unfortunately, as a group, most noise investors lose money. They have one redeeming quality: They do provide increased liquidity for information investors. Information investors understand how financial markets work. They use their financial market knowledge to make money consistently.[1]

In Chapter Eight, we will show you how to become an information investor and calculate your expected returns. This will provide you with a road map to your destination—return enhancement. Does it make any sense to place your hard-earned money in an investment without knowing the range of returns you expect to earn?

Expected return is generally understood to mean the statistically achievable return (based on historical data and future probability assumptions) over a sufficiently long time horizon. Expected returns are theoretical returns; they are not guaranteed future performance measures. However, calculating expected rates of return provides you with a benchmark for determining whether that investment should be made. Second, it allows you to track realized performance and compare it with the expected performance. This allows you to stay on track and know you're on track.

For security analysis, the expected return of a portfolio is the weighted average of all of the expected returns of the investments that make up the portfolio. The expected rate of return is what the prudent investor attempts to maximize at his or her selected level of risk. The success of the strategy is dependent upon the assumptions that were made to calculate the expected return.

DETERMINING FUTURE FINANCIAL OBJECTIVES

All of us have financial goals we're working toward. It could be having enough money to send children or grandchildren to college, having financial independence, or providing for a comfortable retirement. Often these goals change through the years. Your goals will be determined by the dollar amounts you have to invest and the amount of time you have to achieve them.

FIGURE 2–3
Investors' Concerns

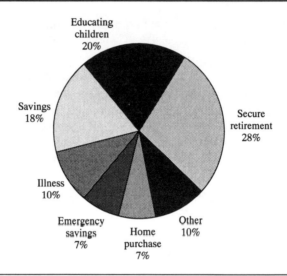

Source: Oppenheimer Funds Distributor, Inc.

A SECURE RETIREMENT

For most investors, the number one goal is having a secure retirement. They want to be able to live comfortably without outliving their money. Investors of all ages share this concern (see Figure 2–3). Can you think of anything more frightening than to be 85 years old, in perfect health, with no money?

In the study reflected in Figure 2-3, investors indicated that securing their retirement was their number one goal, with educating their children a close second. What are your goals?

DEPENDABLE INCOME STREAM

To reach financial independence and retirement goals, you will likely have to develop a dependable income stream, either now or sometime in the future. For this, many investors depend on a single asset class like a savings account, which often guarantees that they'll never reach financial independence. The goal is not only to get a higher rate of return, but at a level of risk that is reasonable and will allow you to stay invested for the long term.

In addition, the income stream you need today is not the income stream you will need tomorrow. Just think: If you were planning your retirement in 1974, you might have budgeted your income needs based on houses that cost $35,000, cars costing less than $5,000, and gas priced at less than 30 cents a gallon. What was a very comfortable income to retire on in 1974 would be a struggle today, unless the income grew to provide for the significantly higher cost of living. Over the last 20 years inflation would have eroded your income by two thirds. Think of how this would have affected your family's lifestyle; the quality of life would have been greatly reduced. Most investors know they need to provide for inflation, but have no idea how to accomplish it. Does your current investment program provide for a dependable income stream?

LIQUIDITY

What if you had an emergency? Without having investment liquidity, you will not be able to respond. Liquidity solves the problem. Liquidity is the ability to realize the value of your holdings through an immediate sale. An effective rule of thumb is that you should have six months worth of living expenses in cash equivalences.

START WITH A CLEAN SHEET OF PAPER

Once you have reviewed your financial needs, you are in a position to design an investment program to meet them. One concept that has recently received a lot of attention in business management circles is process management, which is often referred to as "reengineering." This concept is nothing new. It amounts to knowing where you are, where you want to go, and how you are going to get there, without getting caught up in the distractions.

In building your own investment program, you can use many of these reengineering techniques to get started. The first step is to start with a clean sheet of paper. For the moment, set aside your own biases and what you have read in the popular investment magazines. Remember the printed media's not-so-hidden agenda: They want to sell magazines and advertising space. To accomplish this, they play to the moment. In our office, we call this material "investment pornography," because it gets the reader both excited and confused. To be a successful investor, you must remain skeptical, or maybe a little cynical, of everything you read. Remember what happened the last time you weren't?

So instead of reading what everyone else reads, let's go to the informed sources. We are very fortunate that a tremendous body of empirically tested knowledge has been built by the academic community. These scholars have taken a step back and looked without bias at how investments work. You need to know what they've learned if you are going to succeed.

THE FIVE KEY CONCEPTS OF INVESTMENT SUCCESS

Investing can at times seem overwhelming, but it can be broken down into five simple key concepts. If you examine your own life, it is the simpler things that work consistently. Investing is no different. However, it is easy to have our attention drawn to the wrong issues, and these issues can derail our journey.

Concept 1: Utilize Diversification Effectively to Reduce Risk

Most of us understand the concept of diversification: "Don't put all your eggs in one basket." However, no matter how sophisticated we are, it's easy to get caught in the trap. For instance, many investors have put a large part of their investment capital in their employer's stock, even though they understand that they are probably taking too much risk. They justify their holding due to the large capital gains tax they would have to pay if they withdrew funds, or they imagine that the company is just about to take off. Often it is the only investment they know anything about, and this creates a false sense of comfort.

Our firm's corporate headquarters is in Silicon Valley, where a very high percentage of our clients watched their companies go public and watched themselves become millionaires. Too many do not understand the risk they are taking to maintain their position, rather than diversifying. They could continue to reach their families' financial goals after taxes, if they would only diversify. Unfortunately, some learn of the risks unique to their companies only after the stock has plummeted and they are no longer on track to achieve their financial goals.

Many investment portfolios that are diversified in more than one stock are ineffectively diversified; they concentrate in only one area of the market, such as stocks in large U.S. companies. This sets up the investor for an emotional roller-coaster ride. With only one type of investment, no other investments can help balance the portfolio through tough times. Are your investments concentrated in one area?

To experience the emotions associated with investing, think of the last time a friend or business associate gave you a "hot tip." Did you act on it immediately? Since we're all sophisticated investors, you probably did not buy immediately; like most investors, you are too smart for that. You probably would have called your broker or financial advisor and started following that stock in the paper.

Let's examine how easy it is to get caught on this emotional curve. If this really were a hot stock, one that started trending upward, what would you do? Most investors still would not buy it. At that point, their emotion would be hope. They would be hoping that the stock would continue to go up while they waited for a distinct trend to develop. Let's say it continues to go up; how would emotions change? What would you do?

In many cases, greed would strike. Many investors would have called their broker and purchased the stock. What happens next? Well (as in many hot tips, and in this example), as soon as the stock was purchased, it immediately went down. We are pretty sure that most people reading this book have had this experience. Many investors feel that they can cause a stock's price to go down just by purchasing it. What would your new emotion be? Often it is a combination of fear and hope. What are investors hoping for? They are hoping for the stock to go back up. How far up? To make a profit?

No, if it would just go back up to the price at which they bought it, so they just broke even and wouldn't have to tell their spouses, they would promise never to do it again! But what does the stock do? It often continues going down. And what's the new emotion? Panic. Most investors sell. We are sure that everyone knows what happens next. Some new information comes out and the stock hits an all-time high.

What mistake did the investors in our example make? They bought high and sold low (see Figure 2-4). If you let your emotions get the better of you, serious damage can be done to your investment program.

FIGURE 2–4
The Emotional Curve of Investing

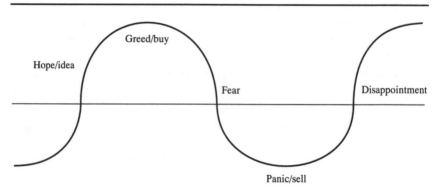

If you're involved in more than one investment but only one type of investment vehicle, such as stocks in large U.S. companies, you're going to fall prey to the emotional curve. All your investments are going to tend to move together.

The overall risk in a portfolio is *not* the average risk of each of the investments; it is actually less if your investments do not move together. By simply including investments in your portfolio that don't move in concert, you can eliminate the specific risk of individual investments that the market does not reward you for. When investments are combined that move differently in time, proportion, and/or direction, you have effective diversification. Dissimilar price movement diversification protects you from having all your investments go down at the same time; it reduces risk. This is a most profound academic investment discovery and represents a dramatic breakthrough in investment methodology.

Examine your current portfolio and try to determine which investments you own today that do not move in tandem. Throughout the book, we will illustrate many different combinations of investments that exhibit this dissimilar price movement. For example, large company and small company stocks tend not to move together.

Concept 2: Dissimilar Price Movement Diversification Enhances Returns

If you have two investment portfolios that have the same average or arithmetic return, the one with the lower volatility will have the greater

FIGURE 2–5
Two Portfolios with the Same Average Rate of Return

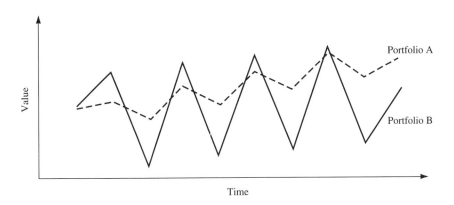

compound or geometric rate of return over time. Let's assume that you have owned two mutual funds with different investment goals for two years. Both have an average annual rate of return of 10 percent. How would you determine which fund was better?

You would expect that the ending value of each mutual fund would be the same, but nothing could be further from the truth. Unless they have the same risk or volatility, that will not happen. If one of the mutual funds took much more risk and was therefore more volatile, their ending values would be significantly different. In Figure 2–5, portfolio A is much less volatile (less up and down movement) than portfolio B and, as a result, has a greater compound rate of return and a higher value at the end of two years. The risk of a portfolio can be less than the average risk of the component investments. To the extent that assets do not move in concert with each other, their specific risks can be diversified away. If two portfolios have the same average return, the one with the lower volatility will have the greater compound rate of return over time. In Figure 2–5, portfolio A has the least volatility. As a result, it has a higher long-term geometric rate of return, and wealth is enhanced.

To use this key concept for investment success, combine investments within a portfolio that move dissimilarly, thus reducing the volatility of the portfolio. Look at the investments that make up your own portfolio. Does the most volatile investment have the highest compound return? Probably not.

Concept 3: Institutional Asset Class Mutual Funds

Many investors who understand the first two concepts attempt to use traditional retail mutual funds to implement them. That's like trying to fix a sink with screwdriver when you really need a pipe wrench. You need the right tools.

Institutional asset class mutual funds are the right tools. It's another term we created to describe mutual funds that were previously only available to institutional investors and consist of index or enhanced-index mutual funds. Institutional investors demand consistency and low cost of operation. Typically, an institutional investor might invest $100 million or more in one of these funds. Due to their large average investments, institutional asset class mutual funds have operating costs less than one-third of the cost of the average no-load U.S. equity mutual fund. We know that controlling costs is one of the few things individual investors can do that enhances the bottom line. In Chapter 6, we examine institutional asset class mutual funds and how you can implement them effectively. Today, over 30 percent of institutional investors utilize these strategies. But, unbelievably, less than 3 percent of America's individual investors are profiting from these simple but effective techniques. Don't be surprised that you haven't heard of them; most investor haven't.

Concept 4: Global Diversification

We've all read of the concept of a "global village"—technology is creating a new paradigm in which businesses around the world are tied together, just as markets are now. (A paradigm is a shared set of assumptions that provide a framework to assist us in predicting behavior.)

From 1965 to 1990, world equity markets grew more than sixfold.[2] While the U.S. market is still the largest equity market, its relative size has decreased significantly relative to the world equity markets as a whole. In building your investment portfolio, you need to consider the world. In 1966, the international equity market was only 29 percent of the total world market; by 1990, it reached 65 percent.[3]

Let's take a look at how two major benchmarks of world performance compare. If we examine Figure 2-6 (the relative performance of U.S. equity markets compared to foreign equity markets from 1970 through 1994), we see long periods of time when the U.S. equity market either outperformed or underperformed foreign markets.

FIGURE 2–6
U.S. and Foreign Markets Perform Differently

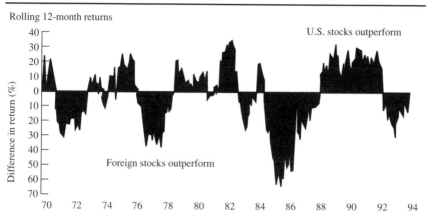

Source: Ibbotson Associates and Morgan Stanley Capital International.

In this graph, the S&P 500 index's rolling 12-month returns were subtracted from Morgan Stanley's Europe Australia Far East (EAFE) index. The EAFE index is comprised of approximately 1,000 large company stocks spread across the world, excluding the United States. Where the shaded area is above the zero line, the U. S. equity market outperformed the foreign markets.

Where the shaded area falls below the zero line, the foreign markets outperformed the U.S. equity market. This is a clear example of dissimilar price movements. Investors who recognize these relationships, are able to protect their investments with confidence over the long term by allocating a portion of their portfolio to foreign markets. This foreign equity exposure will both lower the risk and increase the expected return of your portfolio, as we will see in Chapter 7. With global diversification, investors are insulated from downturns in any one country's market.

Concept 5: Design Portfolios That Are Efficient

How do we decide which investments to utilize, and in what combination? Since 1972, major institutions have been using the money management concept known as Modern Portfolio Theory. It was developed at the

FIGURE 2–7
The Efficient Frontier

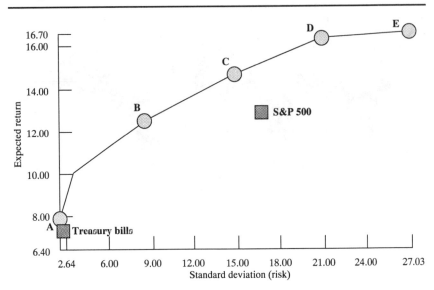

University of Chicago by Harry Markowitz and Merton Miller and later expanded by William Sharpe of Stanford University. Markowitz, Miller, and Sharpe won the Nobel Prize in Economics in 1990 for their investment methodology. The five-step process of developing a strategic portfolio using Modern Portfolio Theory is mathematical in nature and can, at times, appear daunting. It is important to note that math is nothing more than an expression of logic, and as you examine the process, you can readily see the commonsense approach that they have taken, which is counterintuitive to conventional investment thinking.

In Chapter Eight, we will go into more detail about how Modern Portfolio Theory works. To provide a quick overview: Markowitz stated that for every level of risk, there is some optimum combination of investments that will give you the highest rate of return. The components of the portfolio exhibiting this optimal risk/reward trade-off form the "efficient frontier" line. The efficient frontier is determined by calculating the expected rate of return, the standard deviation, and the correlation coefficient for each institutional asset class mutual fund and utilizing this information to optimize the portfolio to get the highest expected return for any given level of risk. By plotting each portfolio representing a given level of risk and expected return, we are able to create a line connecting all efficient portfolios. This line forms the efficient frontier (see Figure 2–7).[4]

Most investor portfolios fall significantly below the efficient frontier. Portfolios such as the S&P 500, which is often used as a proxy for the market, fall below the line when several asset classes are compared. Investors can have same rates of return with an asset class portfolio with much less risk, or they can have higher rates of return for the same level of risk. This shows how you can prudently beat the market. Rational and prudent investors will restrict their choice of portfolios to those that appear on the efficient frontier and to the specific portfolios that represent their own risk-tolerance levels. In Chapter Eight, you will learn how these optimal portfolios are built, and in Chapter Fourteen, you'll see how to implement these concepts so that your portfolio is on the efficient frontier.

Many of these concepts are not widely understood. They represent a new investment paradigm, one shift as important as the telescope was to Galileo. Before you can move to a new paradigm, you have to examine the commonly held set of assumptions that leads to false beliefs. Many investors are making the most important financial decisions of their lives based on incorrect assumptions.

ENDNOTES

[1]Black, Fischer, "Noise," *The Journal of Finance* XLI, no. 3 (July 1986), pp. 529-43. The concepts of noise and informational investors were developed from this article.

[2]Morgan Stanley, *Capital International Perspective,* Geneva, Switzerland.

[3]Morgan Stanley, *Capital International Perspective,* Geneva, Switzerland.

[4]Markowitz, Harry, *The Journal of Finance* 7, no. 1 (March 1952), pp. 77-91.

Chapter Three

From Noise to Information

T his chapter will break through the false beliefs that many noise investors share about investing and start you on the road to becoming a successful information investor. Here is the problem: In most cases, noise is not fact, even when it represents the conventional wisdom of the time. And conventional wisdom is extremely difficult to change. One famous historical example dates from 100 A.D., when Claudius Ptolemy mistakenly placed the earth at the center of the universe. Based on this false belief, he developed a comprehensive system for tracing the motion of the planets and calculated the orbits for each of them. Soon he had an extensive, 13-volume work that was the accepted, authoritative source throughout Europe for over 1,200 years.

Fortunately, Nicholas Copernicus questioned Ptolemy's work, and then formulated his own theory—one that placed the sun at the center of our universe and the earth as a planet rotating around it. His findings showed Ptolemy's ideas to be erroneous. But just as Claudius Ptolemy's work was ultimately questioned and later found to be false, we have learned that many commonly held investment principles are also based on false assumptions. This is very good news. It means there is an easier and more sensible road to investment success.

Galileo used his new invention, the telescope, to show Pope Paul V that Copernicus's theory was accurate—that the earth, in fact, rotates around the sun. But, like many investors today, church officials didn't want to believe what they saw. They warned Galileo to abandon the Copernican system. He did not. Church officials sentenced him to an indefinite prison term.

No one stating new investment truths has been sentenced to prison, but the similarities are obvious. Thousands of people have built careers and businesses around the currently accepted, active investment principles. But the truth is, there is no proven basis for many of the most touted investment beliefs, including the belief that value can be added to an investor's portfolio through stock selection and market timing. These beliefs are, for the most part, a collection of false assumptions. When you finally sift the truth from these faulty paradigms, it's no wonder most people have come to distrust the investment community.

Unfortunately, we cannot accept any new body of knowledge until the chains of our old beliefs are broken. So let's start breaking the chains of these false investment beliefs. Today we have a wealth of data on almost any asset class you can imagine. The advances in technology, particularly the personal computer, have made it easy to collect, manipulate, and study these data. It's hard to believe that 30 years ago there was little to study. There was little time series data available on any asset category. Even the S&P 500 index time series was not readily available.

THE BEGINNING OF AN INVESTMENT PARADIGM SHIFT

The academic community started questioning the financial markets in the early 1900s. The first questions arose when a French mathematician named Louis Bachelier set out to study statistics.[1] While working toward his Ph.D. in mathematics at the University of Paris, Bachelier decided to study the impact of the French futures markets on French government bonds, which traded at the Bourse. He wanted to explore the mathematical properties of these futures, so he examined a series of futures market price changes. He was looking for a statistical relationship between these numbers, to see if there was a way to predict market movements using past trends. This is what every investor would like to do: determine what future price movements will be. If an investor could accomplish this task, untold riches would await him. What Bachelier found was that there was no way to predict the future using these time series data. He found that the historical sequence of price changes provided no information in predicting the next price change. It was a nice piece of work, but it was ignored for 30 to 40 years. His study was lost and never really looked at again until after World War II. However, eventually his work set the stage for the next investigation by academics.

In the 1950s, when the universities and certain research institutions got their hands on computers, researchers naturally wanted to use these tools to analyze data. Some of the first computer applications analyzed returns on stock market indexes and individual stocks and bonds. The academic community began looking at this data with no particular theory or hypothesis in mind, just the desire to learn from what they might discover. But it turned out that a number of academics working in different places—Holbrook Working and Harry Roberts[2] at the University of Chicago, Neil Osborne[3] at IBM Research, and others—all started discovering the same things.

As they examined asset categories, the time series of the price changes was serially uncorrelated. This meant that there was no connection between the previous time series of information and future outcomes. The sequence of a series of rates of return for weekly outcomes, several years of daily outcomes, or a long series of monthly outcomes all appeared to be random. Prior price data uncovered no knowledge of what the next price might be. It was as if the prices were taken from a table of random numbers in the back of a statistics book. A computer generating a series of random, unrelated numbers would have given a similar result. The academic community was beginning to prove the inability to forecast market movements.

Perhaps one of the more interesting of these studies was completed by Harry Roberts, who is professor emeritus of statistics at the University of Chicago Business School. In 1959, rather than doing the esoteric statistical analysis that other academics were doing, he reversed the whole process.[4] He had the computer generate a series of 50 random numbers with a mean of .5 percent and a standard deviation of 2 percent, with a normal distribution (creating a bell-shaped curve). The resulting mean value of plus or minus 2 percent corresponded roughly to the typical weekly price change of the typical stock; that is why he chose those parameters. So he arrived at a series of 50 numbers. Now, obviously, there's no predicted value for these numbers; by their very construction, this series of numbers is empty of content. He then arbitrarily started off with a price of $40 and used the random numbers to develop several graphs that each looked like a series of market changes in a stock price.

Roberts placed a stock name on each chart and went to LaSalle Street in Chicago, which at that time was the world's hotbed for the technical analysis of stocks. He took six or seven of these charts to each of the leading technicians of the day. He introduced himself and asked for advice about how to play the stock market based on this random data. Every one of the technicians had a very strong opinion about what Roberts ought to do with each of these securities.

The patterns that the technicians were observing and speculating about were generated by a computer and were simply the combining of a random series of numbers. There were, by construction, *no* actual patterns, *no* information. When you accumulate random numbers, you get charts that look like patterns. The patterns are in the mind of the viewer; they are not in the data. All of the patterns the technicians saw were easily replicated; they just occur naturally. Roberts wrote his results in a famous article published in 1959 entitled "Stock Market Patterns and Financial Analysis."[5] The technical experts were not amused. Even today, as you flip through the financial channels on television, you will still see technical experts pointing out what the market is going to do next, based on the shape and pattern of the chart. They do not understand how markets work, but it makes entertaining viewing.

Throughout the 60s and early 70s, the focus of most academic work was to determine how efficient markets are. In 1965, Professor Eugene Fama of the University of Chicago wrote his authoritative thesis entitled "The Behavior of Stock Prices" (published in its entirety by the *Journal of Business*), which coined the phrase "efficient markets" and explained how markets appear to be able to fully absorb new information so that all prices of all securities reflect all known information.[6]

The most popular test of that proposition is the examination of mutual fund performance, and the first classic study was presented by Michael Jensen.[7] Jensen looked at the performance of mutual fund portfolios from 1945 to 1964. The managers of these mutual funds were the best and the brightest in the investment community. If anyone possessed special insights about inefficiencies in the market, these experts would. They would also be able to use that information before the rest of the population.

If, on the other hand, markets are efficient and stocks are basically correctly priced at any point in time, the experts won't be able to beat the "naive" strategy of just buying all the securities in the market. Jensen found that the proportion of managers who underperformed the market was significant. The percent of experts with superior positive performance was much lower than you would expect. They were incurring expenses to figure out what stocks were worth, but they were not being compensated by the market for the expenses they were incurring. They were trying to figure out what a stock price was worth when the market was already efficiently determining the right price. Individuals investing in mutual funds whose managers attempt to find inefficiencies in the market have missed the new paradigm.

Jensen stated that there was one source of risk represented in market portfolios. A mutual fund had a higher expected return if it involved more risk than the market. It had a lower expected return if it had less risk than the market. The sensitivity to the market was measured by its *beta*. The beta was determined by a simple regression formula.

Rp	=	Rf + (Rm–Rf)Bp
where Rp	=	Expected return on the portfolio
Rf	=	Risk-free rate of return
Rm	=	Expected rate of return on the market portfolio
Bp	=	Beta for the portfolio

If beta is greater than one, it indicates that this particular asset is much more sensitive to price changes than the market as a whole. Let's say the beta is 1.2 and that the market goes up 10 percent. This would result in an expected price increase of 12 percent for this particular asset. If the market went down 10 percent, this asset would go down 12 percent because it was more sensitive to price changes.

The prevailing theory at the time, the Capital Asset Pricing Model (CAPM), stated that this risk factor was how expected returns were generated. Years earlier, Bill Sharpe and others synthesized beta by adding to Markowitz's work, and they came up with CAPM. For 30 years, CAPM was the methodology used for just about any test that the academic community was doing. Today, many investment advisors still use this work, even though it is outdated.

An article published in *American Economic Review* by Richard Ipolitto in 1964 shocked the academic community. Ipolitto claimed that managers as a group could beat markets and that markets were inefficient—that mutual fund managers could not only take advantage of this inefficiency but were able to beat the market portfolio's performance even after expenses. This was an amazing result with widespread implications. Ipolitto had conducted his study using the same single-factor model as Jensen had, yet he presented opposite results.

Edwin Elton, Martin Gruber, and colleagues completed a review of Ipolitto's work in 1993.[8] Elton and Gruber decided to use Ipolitto's study as the basis of their work. They set out to do their study with the same set of funds. They quickly found out they could not duplicate his results. Why? It turns out that Ipolitto's finding that mutual fund managers had significantly outperformed the market was largely due to data entry errors. He had entered negative returns as positive numbers, but never entered positive returns as negative numbers. All of his mistakes were in favor of the mutual fund managers. So Elton and Gruber corrected these errors, and in the process they wiped out much of the excess performance. Then they looked at small stocks and fixed-income holdings to find out if these factors were important. If they were not important, then the sensitivity of these factors to mutual funds would show up as zero.

Elton and Gruber found that mutual fund managers, on average, not only did not add value, but reduced performance by amounts significantly greater than their fees. They even found that the higher the manager's fees on average, the lower the performance. Of course, paying more for mediocre performance just doesn't make sense.

It is interesting that the popular press gave a lot of attention to the Ipolitto study, when it was first published. Journalists wrote numerous articles stating that markets don't work. The Elton and Gruber study, on the other hand, received little publicity in the popular press. However, it has received a lot of attention in the academic world because it is the most comprehensive mutual fund study completed to date. If anyone is a fan of the idea that markets don't work efficiently, they are not going to enjoy the results of this study.

This is so far the best study available on mutual fund managers, and it comes to the same conclusion that Jensen did 30 years ago. Even though the time periods and mutual funds were so different, the results are strikingly similar. Mutual fund managers who use active management do not just underperform markets, they do so to a significant degree. As an investor, you should not pay fees for something that has been proved not to work.

In 1976, Rex Sinquefield at the American National Bank and his former classmate from the University of Chicago, Roger Ibbotson, published *Stocks, Bonds, Bills, and Inflation (SBBI)*, the first authoritative study of returns and risk profiles of individual asset classes.[9] This was the first widely used tool of time series information on each of the major asset classes made available to the investment community. With computers becoming readily available to the academic and investment communities, the doors were now open to prove what really worked. The introduction of SBBI allowed Sinquefield to establish one of the first institutional asset class mutual funds.

With this new body of knowledge, it became clear that the single-factor model wasn't working. Academics, by focusing only on market risk, were missing the other risk factors that some managers were using to outperform the market portfolio. Managers were getting recognition as adding value through their management techniques, while what they were actually doing was taking different risks that CAPM did not measure.

THE BREAKTHROUGH

It was not until 1992 that Professors Eugene Fama and Kenneth French, both from the University of Chicago, caused the next major breakthrough. Their published article, "The Cross-Section of Expected Stock Returns," expanded Sharpe's single-factor model into a three-factor model that better explains the profit determination of investment portfolios.[10] This landmark research explained over 95 percent of profit determination and illustrated how it was no longer necessary to buy the whole market or individual securities that had higher risk if you were to outperform the market as a whole. Rather, the model developed new asset classes that segmented the market and allowed for superior performance at the same risk as the market as a whole.

Fama and French found that the equity market could be described as having three sources of risk which determined the expected returns.

Market Risk

The first is market risk—the overall market risk that investors participate in through the purchase of equities. Fama and French knew that no one in their right mind would purchase equities over money market funds unless the equities were priced to generate an expected rate of return that would compensate for the overall market risk. This is the same risk factor that Sharpe uncovered in CAPM.

Size Risk

The second source of risk is the size factor. This size factor results in small firms, on average, having higher returns. Small firms are struggling, and the market recognizes that as a source of risk. Given a choice, investors would prefer to own large companies rather than small companies, if both had the same expected returns. Small companies are subject to more volatility, relative to large companies—they don't have the resources to weather downturns. Investors demand a higher expected return for investing in small companies to compensate for this additional risk.

Book-to-Market Risk

The third risk factor is the book-to-market factor. These companies are often struggling in terms of their earnings, but in ways that are different enough from small firms to be considered an independent source of risk. Investors must be compensated for this risk. In Chapter Ten, we will describe in more detail how you can utilize each of the three risk factors to maximize the expected return on your portfolio and easily beat the market. It is due to this work that you are now able to construct prudent portfolios that will outperform market averages by as much as 3 percent.

MARKETS ARE EFFICIENT

It is ironic that one of the most competitive sectors of the market, the financial services industry, is designed to give advice based on the belief that markets do not work. For markets to work, prices have to provide accurate signals for allocating resources. No other pricing system in use today appears better able to allocate resources efficiently than the market system. The rest of the world is embracing the theory that markets are efficient, but many Americans struggle with this issue. We've witnessed the fall of the Soviet Union, Eastern Europe, and many other economies that were centrally planned, due largely to the fact that they were not able to effectively use their resources. Central planning and nonmarket pricing clearly has not worked.

All one needs to do to be a successful information investor is to participate in the free market system's creation of wealth. The ownership of a broadly diversified portfolio of equity securities will accomplish this. Individual companies will attempt to maximize shareholder value. Unfortunately, some won't be successful. On average, they will create tremendous wealth. Your ability to distinguish the losers from the winners is as difficult as picking the winners from the losers.

This chapter described the new investment paradigms. You must shift your own paradigms if you are going to be at the frontier of knowledge.

ENDNOTES

[1]Bachelier, Louis, *Theory of Speculation*, trans. A. James Boness (Paris: Gauthier Villars, 1900). Reprinted in Cootiner.

[2]Roberts, Harry V., "Stock Market Patterns and Financial Analysis: Methodological Suggestions," *Journal of Finance* XIV, no. 1 (March 1959), pp. 1–10.

[3]Osborne, N. F. M., "Brownian Motion in the Stock Market," *Operational Research* 7 (March–April 1959), pp 145–73.

[4]Roberts, Harry V., "Stock Market Patterns and Financial Analysis: Methodological Suggestions," *Journal of Finance* XIV, no.1 (March 1959), pp. 1–10.

[5]Ibid.

[6]Fama, Eugene F., "The Behavior of Stock Prices," *Journal of Business* 37, no. 1 (January 1965), pp. 34–105.

[7]Jensen, Michael C., "The Performance of Mutual Funds in the Period 1945–1964," *Financial Analysts Journal* (November 1989), pp. 587–616.

[8]Ipolitto, Richard, *American Economic Review*, 1964.

[9]Elton, Edwin J.; Martin J. Gruber; Sanjiv Das; and Matthew Hlavka, "Efficiency with Costly Information: A Reinterpretation of Evidence from Managed Portfolios," *The Society for Financial Studies* (1993).

[10]Ibbotson, Roger G. and Rex A. Sinquefield, "Stocks, Bonds, Bills, and Inflation: Year-by-Year Historical Returns (1926–1974)," *Journal of Business* (January 1976), pp. 11–43.

[11]Fama, Eugene F. and Kenneth R. French, "The Cross-Section of Expected Stock Returns," *Journal of Finance* (June 1993), pp 427–65.

Chapter Four

Effective Diversification

I f you brought this book to your local stockbroker and dropped it on the desk, she or he may dismiss its premise, saying, "All they are talking about is passive investing through index funds and I can show you how to do much better through active management." But your stockbroker would be wrong. It's nothing personal; most investment firms teach conventional investment wisdom. In fact, 97 percent of the retail mutual funds use active management techniques of market timing and stock selection. They sell mutual funds.

But every major academic study of passive versus active money management states that, on average, passive investing will significantly outperform active investing. Active money management attempts to predict the future through estimating the timing of financial market turns and identifying good stocks. Passive money management doesn't believe this is possible. Passive money management utilizes index mutual funds to replicate market averages. And it's the averages that consistently outperform active strategies.

Probability theory suggests that there will always be some money manager who will outperform a purely passive approach (someone has to win the lottery). But it's equally difficult to identify ahead of time who is going to win either the active management game or the lottery.

We have taken traditional, passive management strategies several steps further. By using a series of institutional asset class mutual funds, we will outperform a purely passive management strategy. We will show you how to take the best from the passive strategy and then add to it, without being active. In Chapter Six, we will fully describe these institutional asset class mutual funds. Then in Chapter Thirteen we will show how Asset Class Investing will significantly outperform both active and passive strategies.

In this chapter, you will learn how to use the first key concept of Asset Class Investing–effective diversification, which reduces your risk of investing. You will discover that one of the significant differences between effective and ineffective diversification is the passive versus active argument.

First, let's take a step back and examine how markets really work. This knowledge will allow you to capture higher returns with less risk. Stock prices are based on all known information. Today's stock prices reflect up-to-date information. The belief that you can get unreflected information from a stockbroker is a false assumption. It sets you up for dependence and failure. You don't need the stockbroker's opinion. All you need to do to participate in the free market system is to own equities, because companies as a whole have one underlying goal in common, and that is to maximize shareholder value. And they are going to do everything possible to achieve that goal. It is in their best interests to do so. Instead of trying to pick which stock is going to be successful, if an investor did nothing more than own the market, he or she would participate in its growth.

Today, at most major institutional firms, a manager can easily move a billion dollars with the push of a button, and will, if that move can gain an eighth-of-a-point advantage for clients. Each market participant acts independently with significant resources, both capital and information, forcing prices to reflect all known information. Today's price is the best indicator of the value of a stock. The truth is, however, that as good as Wall Street is at valuing stock given today's information, it can't predict the future. Asset managers can't pick individual stocks with any consistency, based on past performance. They cannot tell you when the market is going to go up or when it is going to go down.

Frequently, investors are guilty of believing that someone can predict the future and assist them with their investment decisions. These investors want to believe that stock prices can be predicted through techniques known either as technical or fundamental analysis.[1] The academic community has proved that these techniques add little or no value. In a 1953 study, Maurice Kendall concluded that stock prices follow a random walk and are thus unpredictable as long as investors share all relevant information about the stock in question.[2]

One could liken a random walk to a coin-flipping contest. It is widely believed that the law of averages ensures that in a long coin-tossing game, each player will be on the winning side about half the time, with the lead passing frequently from one player to the other. When a coin is flipped 10,000 times, one would think that the lead would change hands every second or third flip, but statistically we should expect this shift to happen only 100 times. Contrary to popular belief, the laws governing a prolonged series of coin flips show patterns and averages far removed from those expected. If a simple coin-tossing game leads to paradoxical results that contradict our intuition, then our intuition cannot possibly serve as a reliable guide in the more complicated securities market.

In Figure 4–1, we utilized a random-number generator in our computer to simulate what might happen with 10,000 coin tosses. (We couldn't find any volunteers to do it.) When you examine the resulting graph, you may be surprised by the length of the interludes between successive passes across the axis.

The graph illustrates clearly how a coin toss is a random act with random results; we know that future directions cannot be predicted on the basis of past information. However, the graph bears a surprising resemblance to movements in the securities markets. Remember that in flipping a coin, the expected rate of return is zero; for you to win, the other person has to lose. In the financial markets, however, that is not the case. The average annual compounded rate of return for the last 68 years in the S&P 500 has been 10.3 percent. If we had sloped the graph with a rate of return of 10 percent, it would look very much like the typical performance of the stock market as a whole—and many soothsaying technicians would have been able to tell us exactly where the market was going to go. It would have looked exactly like a typical stock price movement pattern.

Figure 4–1 illustrates clearly how a coin toss is a random walk, in which future directions cannot be predicted on the basis of past information. There is no information to perceive in the sequence. Since the coin-tossing results appear similar to securities price movements, we must question whether anyone is able to gain knowledge of securities markets if they are subject to this random walk.

If you flip a coin, you know that about half the time it's going to come up heads and half the time it's going to come up tails. But if you consistently flipped heads for a period of time, it doesn't tell you anything about the next flip. You are just as likely to flip heads again instead of tails.

The effect of not being able to predict future price movements from past information is known as a random walk. From another point of view, it can be likened to a drunken sailor; he is just as likely to show up where he started or a mile down the road—there is no way to predict where he's going to go. In the financial markets, random walk means that you cannot determine by past price movements what's going to happen next. The drunken sailor cannot predict himself where he's going to end up, so how can anyone else? The markets are the same in the short run.

FIGURE 4–1
Results of 10,000 Coin Tosses

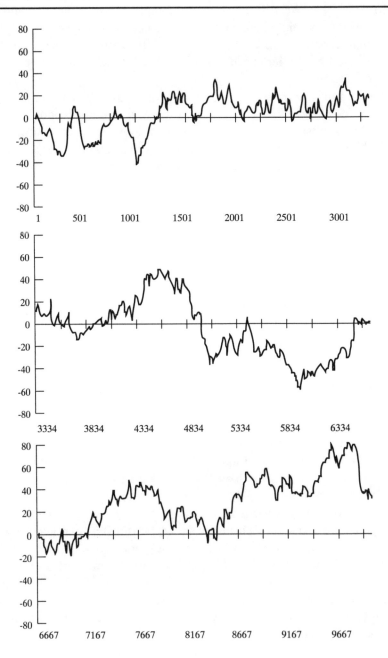

Ever since the results of Kendall's study were released, controversy has surrounded his random walk hypothesis. A strict interpretation of Kendall's results would imply that no technique of stock portfolio selection can consistently outperform a simple buy-and-hold strategy, utilizing a broadly diversified group of securities. In other words, the most popular market indexes, which represent broad segments of the marketplace, will outperform the majority of professional money managers on a consistent basis.

According to former Princeton University Professor Burton Malkiel, "a blindfolded chimpanzee throwing darts at the stock pages of *The Wall Street Journal* could select a portfolio that performs as well as one carefully chosen by the experts." The truth is, no one can predict the future, as much as many people try to convince you that they can. They cannot pick individual securities with any consistency, based on past performance. What we are saying is that past information doesn't tell you anything about future performance. The Securities and Exchange Commission requires all offerings to state to the public that "past performance is no indicator of future performance." Nothing could be more true.

WHAT ABOUT MUTUAL FUND MANAGERS?

Are mutual fund managers able to beat the market? John Bogle, chairman and chief executive officer of the Vanguard Group of investment companies, addressed the No-Load Mutual Fund Enterprise Conference in Chicago in June 1991. The title of his speech was, "Why Is It Virtually Impossible to Pick the Winners, Yet So Easy to Pick a Winner?" The conclusion reached by CEO Bogle is significant and somewhat surprising, since he represents a company with one of the best-known, actively managed funds in the marketplace. He states that a "passive market strategy will, under all circumstances, past and future alike, outperform the combined results of all active strategies in the aggregate." He also went on to say that, "the relative return achieved by an equity mutual fund yesterday has virtually no material predictive value for tomorrow." He offered the data in Tables 4–1 and 4–2 as evidence to support these theories.

Mutual funds using both market timing and stock selection that have been in the top 20 in a given year have, on average, ranked 284th out of 681 funds in the subsequent year. If they ranked in the top 20 over a span of 10 years, their rank, on average, fell to 142nd out of 309 funds during the subsequent 10 years. Past performance of mutual funds has not been an accurate measure of future performance. Bogle's comments and statistics seem to further support the random walk theory.

Have institutional money managers been rewarded in their quest to beat the market? A recent study published in the *Financial Analysts Journal* examined that question by contrasting the random walk theory with active management. It illustrated how shifting asset weights introduces uncertainty. The researcher invested randomly in the S&P 500 and Treasury bonds on a monthly basis.

In essence, when the coin came up heads, they invested 65 percent in the S&P 500 and 35 percent in Treasury bonds for that month, and when the coin turned up tails, they invested 35 percent in the S&P 500 and 65 percent in Treasury bonds for that month. The returns from the strategy obviously depended on coin-flipping probabilities. To estimate the outcomes of 1,000 money managers, 1,000 trials were randomly run over a simulated period of five years. They flipped the coin 60 times to simulate the 60 months during 1986 through 1990. It was as though 1,000 managers were actively engaged in a market-timing contest. Table 4–3 shows that the average return, or benchmark performance, was 12.52 percent with a normal distribution realized.

The institutional portfolios behaved very similarly to the randomly generated portfolios (Table 4-4). Ten percent of the funds have returns some 200 basis points per year above the median, and 10 percent of the funds have returns that are 200 basis points per year below the median.

TABLE 4–1
One-Year Rank Order of Top 20 Equity Funds (1982–92)

First-Year Rank	Average Rank in Subsequent Years	First-Year Rank	Average Rank in Subsequent Years
1	100	11	310
2	383	12	262
3	231	13	271
4	343	14	207
5	358	15	271
6	239	16	287
7	220	17	332
8	417	18	348
9	242	19	310
10	330	20	226

Average rank of top 20 in subsequent years = 284.
Average number of funds = 681.

TABLE 4–2
Ten-Year Rank Order of Top 20 Equity Funds*

Rank 1972–82	Rank 1982–92	Rank 1972–82	Rank 1982–92
1	128	11	222
2	34	12	5
3	148	13	118
4	220	14	228
5	16	15	205
6	2	16	78
7	199	17	209
8	15	18	237
9	177	19	119
10	245	20	242

Average rank of top 20 in subsequent decade = 142.
Average number of funds = 309.
*Concentrated specialty and international funds excluded.

The 400-basis-point spread of returns between the 10th and 90th percentiles simply measures the uncertainty introduced by active management.

Investors should have expected a significant premium over the benchmark performance for the additional uncertainty in active management. However, active management, on average, significantly underperformed the benchmark returns. By contrast, the benchmark portfolios reliably increased the portfolio's compound returns through the diversification process and eliminated benchmark risk—the risk of differing from your measure of performance.

TABLE 4–3
Distribution of Random Portfolio

10th percentile	14.33
50th percentile	13.39
90th percentile	10.52
Spread, 10–90th percentile	3.81
Benchmark portfolio performance	12.52
S&P 500 portfolio	13.14
Treasury bills	10.74

Source: David G. Booth and Eugene F. Fama, "Diversification Returns and Asset Contributions," *Financial Analysts Journal* (May/June 1992).

TABLE 4–4
Distribution of Institutional Portfolio

10th percentile	12.38
50th percentile	10.47
90th percentile	8.35
Spread, 10th–90th percentile	4.03

Source: SEI Corporation.

Once you know that all information is reflected in current prices of individual securities, you are free to focus on what really adds value to your portfolio, rather than chasing individual security selection or market timing. By building a portfolio that includes the market as a whole, you can capture market returns and avoid the additional costs associated with market timing and superior stock selection.

AN ISLAND ECONOMY

When you begin to build your portfolio, you will need effective diversification. Nobel laureate Merton Miller, when asked to sum up the most important investment concept individuals should know, stated, "Diversification is your buddy." To utilize diversification effectively, you must recognize that markets are indeed efficient. Once you have realized that this efficiency exists, then you can move on to discover how diversification really works.

An example comes from Burton Malkiel's 1973 book, *A Random Walk Down Wall Street*.6 Malkiel illustrates the theory brilliantly in a story about an island economy. On this island is a large resort and a manufacturing firm that makes umbrellas. Weather affects the fortunes of both. During sunny seasons, the resort does a booming business, but umbrella sales plummet. During rainy seasons, the resort owner does very poorly, while the umbrella manufacturer enjoys high sales and large profits.

Table 4–5 shows a hypothetical comparison of the two businesses during different seasons.

Suppose that, on average, one half of the seasons are sunny and one half are rainy (i.e., the probability of a sunny or rainy season is one half). An investor who bought stock in the umbrella manufacturer would find that half the time he earned a 50 percent return and half the time he lost 25

TABLE 4–5
Seasonal Fluctuations for Two Businesses

Season	Umbrella Manufacturer	Resort Owner
Rainy	50%	-25%
Sunny	-25%	50%

percent of his investment. On average, he would earn a return of 12.5 percent. This is called the investor's expected return. Similarly, investment in the resort produces the same results. The story points out that investing in either one or the other of these businesses would be more risky than investing in equal amounts of each.

Here's where the diversification angle comes into the story. The author has his hypothetical investor invest half his money in the umbrella manufacturing business and half in the resort. Now, during the sunny seasons, a $1 investment in the resort would produce a 50-cent return, while a $1 investment in umbrella manufacturing would result in a 25-cent loss. The investor's total return would be 25 cents (50 cents minus 25 cents), which is 12.5 percent of his total investment of $2.

The same thing happens during rainy seasons, except that the names are changed. Investment in the umbrella company produces a good 50 percent return, while investment in the resort results in a 25 percent loss. The advantage happens when there is a freak year–it rains all year or is sunny all year. If the investor put all his money in the resort and it rained all year, he might have a 100 percent loss. But in Malkiel's diversified model, the investor makes a 12.5 percent return on his total investment nonetheless.

This simple illustration points out the advantage of diversification. No matter what happens to the weather, and thus to the island economy, by diversifying investments between both of the firms, an investor is making a 12.5 percent return each year. The trick that makes the game work is that, while both companies are risky (returns are variable from season to season), the companies were affected differently by the weather's covariance. Covariance measures the degree to which two risky assets move in tandem. A positive covariance indicates that asset returns move together, while a negative covariance means they vary inversely. As long as there is some lack of parallelism in the fortunes of the individual companies in the economy, diversification will always reduce risk.

Portfolios of volatile stocks might be put together in a similar way. The portfolio as a whole would actually be less risky than any one of the individual stocks in it. It is the negative covariance that plays the critical role in the successful management of institutional stock portfolios; negative covariance is the most academically sound approach to diversifying the risks out of your portfolio.

DIVERSIFYING THE U.S. AND JAPANESE EQUITY MARKETS

Consider the case of investing in Japanese stocks. In late 1992, the Nikkei Index plummeted to 14,309, representing a six-year low for the volatile Japanese stock market. Looking back at this period with the benefit of 20-20 hindsight, we would assume that investment portfolios that stayed out of the Japanese market entirely would have performed better than those that diversified using Japanese stocks. Investing entirely in U.S. stocks would have been a lot better or would it? Perhaps this is one time that diversification would have failed to serve us well. Before you dismiss our theory so quickly, however, let's examine the data more carefully.

First, let's review the results of a portfolio that invested 50 percent in the S&P 500 index and 50 percent into a portfolio of U.S. small company stocks. We simulated the performance of this all-U.S. portfolio from May 1, 1987, through April 30, 1993, a time of general decline in the Japanese stock market. We assumed an annual rebalancing in each example. The results for a portfolio indicate a 9.1 percent annualized rate of return. The one-year standard deviation for this all-U.S. portfolio is 9.8 percent.

Next, we simulated the same type of portfolio mix within the Japanese market. That is, we invested 50 percent in Japanese large company stocks and 50 percent in Japanese small company stocks. This all-Japanese portfolio generated an annualized return of 6.7 percent, with a one-year standard deviation of 33.4 percent. With a lower rate of return than the U.S. stocks and a higher standard deviation, why would we possibly advocate diversifying to include these Japanese investments in our portfolio?

In Figure 4–2 we've compared these portfolios to a mixture consisting of 75 percent invested in the U.S. portfolio and 25 percent invested in the Japanese market. You'll note that the combined 9.6 percent annualized rate of return was higher than that of either component. In addition, the standard deviation of the blended portfolio dropped to 8.8 percent. Even though the Japanese market underperformed the U.S. equities, diversifying with Japanese stocks enhanced the returns of the U.S. stocks while also lowering volatility. How is this phenomenon possible?

The answer is very simple. Negative covariance or low correlation between these markets has smoothed out the ride and enhanced overall performance. The purchase of asset classes possessing low correlation among them is the Nobel Prize-winning secret for achieving better portfolio consistency. The search for asset classes having negative covariances or low correlations is a fundamental principle.

What do we mean by "low correlation"? First, let's look at the meaning of correlation. Correlation is a statistical measure of the degree to which the movement of two variables is related. Correlation measurements range from +1.000 (perfect positive correlation) to −1.000 (perfect negative correlation). When two assets have a +1.000 correlation, they move up and down at the same time, with the same magnitude. There is no diversification advantage to be gained by pairing two assets with a +1.000 correlation. On the other hand, pairing assets having a −1.000 correlation would be advantageous.

The advantage of building a portfolio with assets having low correlation is that one asset is likely to rise when another is falling. Thus, the combined portfolio will be less susceptible to volatility than the individual assets. In constructing your portfolio, it is critical to include asset classes with low correlation coefficients. The power in properly utilizing correlation coefficients to construct well-diversified portfolios has been well documented. The results are very compelling.

The measurement of correlation and the utilization of asset classes having low correlations are fundamental ingredients in the Asset Class Investing process. The principle of diversification offers greater comfort to the long-term investor because each kind of investment follows its own market cycle. Each asset responds differently to changes in the economy or the investment marketplace. If you own a variety of assets, a short-term decline in one asset class can be balanced by others that are stable or are experiencing a positive return. The key is to search out and find groups of investment assets that do not move together in unison, but rather move inversely or dissimilarly.

While some investors can tolerate the higher risk associated with non-diversification, most cannot. Suppose you had invested all your money in stocks and you needed to sell some of your holdings for an emergency. If

FIGURE 4–2
Comparison of Three Portfolio Mixes

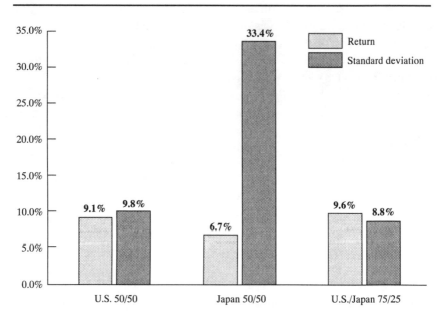

stock prices were depressed at the time you needed to sell, you might be forced to take a loss on your investment. Owning other types of investments would give you more flexibility in raising the needed cash, while allowing you to hold your stocks until prices improved. While money market funds provide liquidity and low risk, their overall return was more than 75 percent less for the 10-year period ending December 1994 than the return from a diversified portfolio. A reduced return of this magnitude is a high price to pay for perceived investment stability. A diversified portfolio, on the other hand, provides both liquidity and comparative stability.

Diversification is a prudent method for managing certain types of investment risk. Unsystematic risks, such as management risks, competitive risks, and finance risks, can be reduced through diversification. However, this is not effective if all the assets are invested in the same market segment or in market segments that tend to move in tandem. If all investments were to decrease in value at the same time, that type of diversification would be ineffective (see Figure 4–3). For instance, one could own a representative equivalent of the S&P 500 and the Dow Jones

Industrial Average. Since both tend to move in the same direction at the same time, this would not be effective diversification.

FIGURE 4–3
Ineffective Diversification

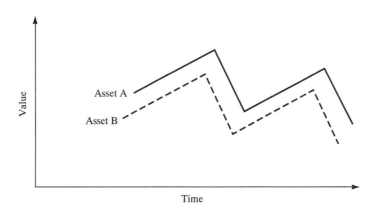

FIGURE 4–4
Effective Diversification

While all diversification is good, certain types of diversification are
. better. This was the premise of Markowitz's theory. He showed that, to the
extent that securities in a portfolio do not move in concert with each other,
their individual risks can be effectively diversified away (see Figure 4–4).

FIGURE 4–4
Effective Diversification

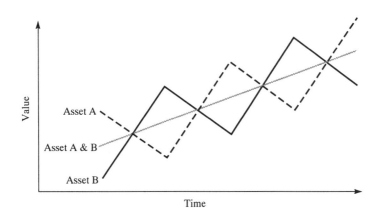

Effective diversification reduces extreme price fluctuations and smooths out returns. This can best be accomplished through the use of asset class mutual funds.

Over the long term, owning a wide variety of investments is the best strategy for the investor trying to achieve investment success. But which investments are right for you?

ENDNOTES

[1]Technical analysis is the attempt to identify mispriced securities and focuses on stock market patterns. Fundamental analysis is the attempt to predict future stock prices based on such determinants as earnings, dividends, and other risk factors. Wall Street reinforces and benefits from the continuation of these false beliefs.

[2]Kendall, Maurice G., "The Analysis of Time Series, Part I: Prices," *Journal of the Royal Statistical Society* 96 (1953), pp 11–25.

[3]Malkiel, Burton G., *A Random Walk Down Wall Street.* New York: Norton & Company, 1973.

[4]Bogle, John C., *Bogle on Mutual Funds.* Chicago: Irwin Professional Publishing, 1994.

[5]Booth, David G. and Eugene F. Fama, "Diversification Returns and Asset Contributions," *Financial Analysts Journal* (May–June 1992).

[6]Malkiel, Burton G., *A Random Walk Down Wall Street.* New York: Norton & Company, 1973.

Chapter Five

Dissimilar Price Movements Enhance Investment Returns

I n the last chapter we discussed how effective diversification uses dissimilar price movements to reduce risk. This chapter will illustrate how dissimilar price movements enhance returns—the second key concept.

A landmark academic discovery that resulted in a dramatic breakthrough for investment management methodology can assist the investor in determining which combination of investments she or he should own. The discovery was this: When two portfolios have the same arithmetic rate of return, the portfolio with smaller up-and-down swings in value (less volatility) will have the greater geometric compound rate of return over time. Because asset class portfolios combine asset classes that do not move together—that is, they have dissimilar price movements—the volatility of the portfolio can be significantly reduced. Consequently, your prospects for a greater compound rate of return over time are enhanced. This reduction in volatility also allows you to focus on the long term, rather than being distracted by the mixed messages that the media broadcasts each day.

Harry Markowitz showed that, for a given expected return, reducing a portfolio's variance increases the compound rate of return.[1] For example, a $100 portfolio that is up 20 percent in one period and unchanged in a second period has $120 after the two periods. If we reduce the portfolio's variance to zero (up 10 percent the first period and up 10 percent the second period), we maintain our average rate of return (10 percent) but end up with $121 after the two periods. If two portfolios have the same arithmetic expected return, the one with the lower volatility will have the greater geometric compound rate of return (see Figure 5–1).

This phenomenon of variance is indifferent to market direction. Although absolute variance reduction requires underperformance during certain periods, it ultimately assures a higher compound rate of return.

FIGURE 5–1
Two Portfolios With the Same Average Rate of Return

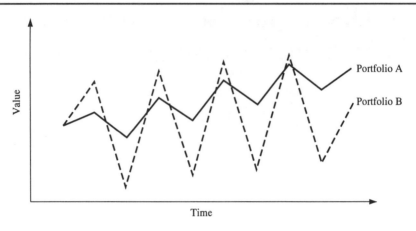

It is very similar to the concept of the tortoise and the hare, where the hare is racing like crazy, but all over the place; yes, he does eventually get there, but the tortoise is slow and steady and wins the race in the end.

One of the most significant values that Asset Class Investing brings to portfolio management is minimizing risk through volatility reduction. Unfortunately, most money managers do not focus on risk management, even though it is recognized as one of the key ingredients of investment success. Let's take a further look at the negative consequences of high portfolio volatility and suggest how to manage this volatility better.

Risk management is one of the keys to investment success. Unfortunately, many investors find it difficult to understand. Effective risk management is the measurement and control of portfolio volatility. By demonstrating how higher portfolio volatility can cause lower rates of return, we hope to create a better understanding of the role that all these terms play in successful investing.

Let's take a look at an example. From 1975 through 1994, ABC Company stock rose 15 percent per year with no volatility. The standard deviation of ABC was zero. During this same 20-year period, XYZ Company stock averaged 15 percent per year by recording alternate years of +35 percent and -5 percent, a 20 percent swing each way from the 15 percent average. Did ABC and XYZ stocks finish the 20-year period with the same compound rate of return?

At first glance we answer, "Yes. Of course. Both stocks had an average rate of return of 15 percent per year." However, the correct answer may surprise you. The volatility of XYZ Company stock cost its investors dearly by the end of the 20th year. Figure 5–2 shows the changes to both investment accounts, with each stock position initially having a market value of $10,000.

FIGURE 5–2
Comparison of Volatile and Nonvolatile Stocks

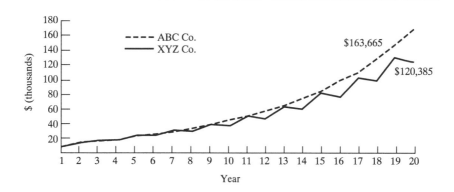

The high volatility of XYZ Company stock cost its investors $43,280 over this 20-year period. The ABC Company stock investment compounded at 15 percent per year. However, the XYZ stock compounded at only a 13.25 percent rate due to its volatility. The lower volatility of ABC stock created a higher compound rate of return.

The complete elimination of portfolio volatility is virtually impossible. How much would the volatility of XYZ stock need to be decreased to improve our rate of return? Let's assume that we were able to reduce the volatility by either 25, 50, or 75 percent. In other words, the returns would vary between 0 and 30 percent, between 5 and 25 percent, or between 10 and 20 percent, respectively. How would these reductions in volatility affect our compound rate of return? The results are summarized in Table 5–1.

It is important to note that each percentage improvement in the rate of return is greater than the corresponding percentage decrease in portfolio volatility. In other words, a 25 percent decrease in volatility creates a 44 percent improvement in our rate of return. Instead of a 1.75 percent decrease in rate of return caused by 20 percent volatility swings, we experience only a 0.98 percent decrease, a 44 percent improvement.

TABLE 5–1
Increases in Rates of Return with Decreasing Volatitlity

	Volatility Reduction %	Annual Returns %	Increased Principal in 20 Years $	Compound Rate of Return % (N)	Difference in Volatility (15% - N)	Increased Annualized Return %	Percent Improved %
XYZ Co.	0	-5 to 35	0	13.25	1.75	—	—
	25	0 to 30	17,473	14.02	0.98	0.77	44
	50	5 to 25	31,317	14.56	0.44	1.31	75
	75	10 to 20	40,212	14.89	0.11	1.64	94
ABC Co.	100	15	43,280	15.00	0.00	1.75	100

This example clearly illustrates the risk associated with high volatility. The next time you're considering two portfolios with similar expected rates of return, you'll realize the importance of selecting the one with the lower expected volatility. Focusing on portfolio volatility in this manner is simply considered to be prudent risk management. The realization that two portfolios have the same mathematical rate of return but have different volatilities, which means different ending values of wealth, puts you on the road to success. The portfolio with the lower volatility will have a higher ending value of wealth over time. All investors are interested in maximizing their ending wealth value. Lower volatility not only improves our wealth, but our investment comfort level as well. This allows an investor to ride through the inevitable downturns.

By combining asset classes with low correlations, you can lower portfolio volatility while enhancing risk-adjusted rates of return. The use of low and/or negative correlation is a powerful tool in providing effective diversification. By using asset classes to represent whole market segments, the essence of Markowitz's efficient portfolio theory has now been brought to a higher level. The recent increases in the speed of computers have made it possible to make millions of computations to aid in the selection of individual securities for market segment funds called institutional asset classes (see Chapter Six). The resulting funds are useful diversification tools and can achieve much safer dissimilar-price-movement diversification because they are, in themselves, diversified.

Computer simulations using historical data show that when asset classes having dissimilar price movements are combined, Asset Class Investing is superior to the two other investment methodologies, marketing timing or stock selection. Studies indicate that asset class portfolios outperform, in total returns, 75 percent of institutional plans that use market timing and stock selection methodologies when invested over time horizons in excess of five years. Asset Class Investing reduces risk and simultaneously enhances compounded rates of return.

THREE INVESTMENT METHODOLOGIES AND THEIR EFFECTS ON VOLATILITY

The first methodology, security selection, centers on the belief that diligent research will uncover pricing inefficiencies that can be taken advantage of to gain excess profits. However, the markets are highly efficient, as we have discussed, due to the abundance of very bright and capable investment analysts and the instantaneous flow of information now possible with high-tech communications. Today, computers and modems, faxes, and telecommunications enable us to send and analyze data instantly. If markets are efficient, and they appear to be, each security is sold at the correct price based on all available information. Security selection cannot enhance results consistently and reliably. Again, numerous studies have shown that, on average, a person (or a chimpanzee) throwing darts at a stock listing can create a portfolio that performs as well as one created by a professional analyst.

FIGURE 5–3
Percentage of Money Managers Beating the S&P 500

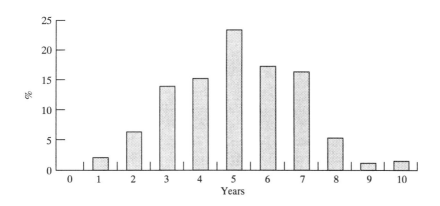

SEI Research, using its equity fund database, showed that on a before-fee basis, "the odds are better of finding a coin flipper who can consistently flip 'heads' than they are of finding a manager who can consistently beat the S&P 500." [2]As reported in "Investing in Small Capitalization Stocks 1926-1990," Dimensional Fund Advisors, Inc., February 1991, p.13. What is surprising is that we have actually found fewer managers beating the market averages than we would expect from mere chance (see Figures 5–3 and 5–4). Studies have further shown that stock selection strategies may actually reduce rates of return and increase portfolio risk because little attention is given to effective diversification.

The analysts' greatest disadvantage is their combined salary and trading costs, which are significant and have to be made up before their portfolios can even compete with the index averages that they are trying to beat. Investment professionals have not been able to consistently outperform the random selection of stocks.

FIGURE 5–4

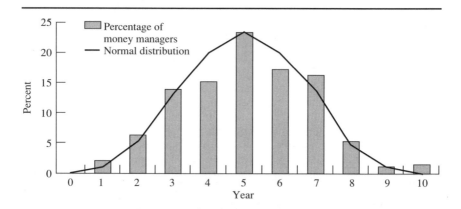

The second methodology, market timing, is an attempt to switch from an equity position to a cash position when a bear (down) market in stocks is forecasted, and then back into the market when a bull (up) market is anticipated. In a free market, the market values of the market itself and of each of its many component securities reflect all known information. Future changes in value will only occur when new changes or events happen, and the results of these are unpredictable. No major academic study has indicated that market timing works. Market timers are, in essence, saying that a security or a whole market can be mispriced and may not properly reflect its current and/or future value. While it may be arguable that at times one individual stock is mispriced, it appears highly unlikely that whole segments of the market are mispriced. No one has successfully and consistently been able to foretell the change in the value of the Dow Jones average one day in advance, let alone one month or one year in advance.

A study of 100 large pension plans showed that while all the funds had engaged in at least some market timing, not one of the funds had improved its rate of return as a result.[2] In fact, 89 of the 100 lost value as a result of market timing. One study determined that market timers must have a 91 percent forecasting accuracy to beat a buy-and-hold strategy.[3] Another study showed that in the period from 1980 to 1989, if the market timer were in cash during the 40 best days, the return would have been reduced to only 3.9 percent, while the return of a buy-and-hold strategy on the S&P 500 was 17.9 percent.[4] Robert Jeffrey showed, after studying mutual fund results from the years 1926 to 1982, that the maximum downside risk from market timing was twice the maximum upside potential.[5] Statistically, reliance on market timing is dangerous because it does not produce consistent results and does not provide the risk protection required for an investor's life savings.

FIGURE 5–5
Determinants of Portfolio Performance

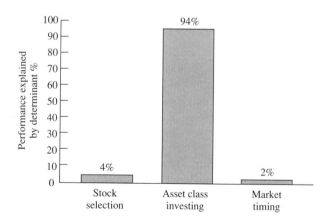

The third methodology, Asset Class Investing, combines various asset classes such as stocks, bonds, and cash equivalents in an effective diversification. This differs from what most investors think of as diversification—owning a large range of individual stocks and bonds. By focusing on broad diversification of asset classes, risk is reduced and the expected return is enhanced. This is accomplished without reliance on inconsistent market timing or security selection methods. Before Harry Markowitz published his award-winning theory, the risk for an asset allocation fund was believed to equal the average risk for the component securities in the portfolio. But, as Markowitz points out, to the extent that the component parts of the portfolio move in the same direction, this diversification may not be effective. Three separate studies of 91 large pension plans over two different 10-year periods show that asset class selection accounts for more than 94 percent of investment results and is clearly the most important investment decision made (see Figure 5–5).[6]

If all the major academic studies indicate that the allocation of investments in asset classes with dissimilar price movements is the answer to investment success, it seems prudent to use this method. Let's see how we can use asset classes to build a portfolio for retirement, and let's look at this method's effect on the quality of life of an investor's family.

In Table 5–2, we illustrate a conservative, asset class portfolio. We have seven asset classes, one half in bond asset classes and one half in equity. We will show you how this portfolio was constructed in Chapter Eight. In Figure 5–6, we have simulated how an asset class portfolio invested at the conservative risk level would have performed during this time period when measured against one of the top-performing portfolios, the S&P 500. We have labeled our model portfolios defensive, conservative, moderate, and aggressive, based on their respective percentage in the stock market. These labels are somewhat misleading because there are no standard definitions. Our aggresive portfolio has about the same risk as the S&P 500 index, but many investment advisors would not consider the S&P 500 index aggressive at all. Don't get caught up with what type of investor you are; in Chapter Eight we will help you identify which portfolio is most appropriate for you.

For the 23-year period from January 1, 1972, through December 31, 1994, U.S. Treasury bills earned an average annual compound rate of return of 7.1 percent. During this same period, the S&P 500 index earned 11.1 percent and the simulated return for the conservative asset class portfolio was 14.1 percent. With less than 50 percent of the asset class portfolio in equities, it outperformed the S&P 500 with less risk. Dissimilar price movement diversification does work.

Note that the asset class account did better than the S&P 500 for this time period, but what about shorter periods? Will your asset class account always outperform the market? Of course not.

TABLE 5–2
Conservative Portfolio

Money market fund	5%
One–year fixed	20%
Five–year government	25%
U.S. large companies	20%
U.S. small companies	5%
International large companies	20%
International small companies	5%
Portfolio Total	100%

These results lead us to believe that the safest way to invest for a steady income and still have our investment portfolio grow is to utilize the asset class portfolio, with the S&P 500 a close second and Treasury bills far behind.

FIGURE 5–6
Conservative vs. S&P 500 and Treasury Bills, 1972–1994

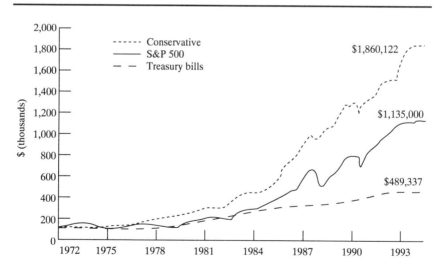

In Figure 5–7, we assume that you invested $100,000 in each of three alternatives (Treasury bills, S&P 500, and the conservative portfolio) and that you withdrew $2,000 per quarter from each investment for 22 years. This annual withdrawal rate (8 percent of your original investment) seems reasonable. Let's examine the results.

Figure 5–7 shows quite graphically that the Treasury bills present the greatest problem for an income investor because they fail to earn returns at a high enough rate to pay out 8 percent per year. The initial investment of $100,000 falls to $47,356, and this is before adjusting for inflation and taxes! The investment in the S&P 500 does better by netting a $117,933 balance in the account after removing $184,000 through quarterly distributions. The best performance, by a substantial margin, belongs to the conservative account, which also has much lower risk. After withdrawing the same $184,000, the conservative account is left with a balance of $666,464! This is a 565 percent improvement in the ending capital balance when compared to the S&P 500.

FIGURE 5–7
Conservative vs. S&P 500 and Treasury Bills
(Less Quarterly Income of $2,000), 1972–1994

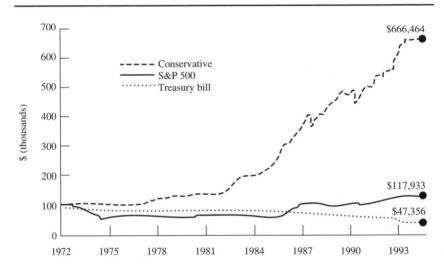

Why is there such a dramatic difference between the conservative portfolio and the S&P 500, when their rates of return were similar? The answer is that the lower volatility of a portfolio of dissimilar-price-movement asset classes prevents it from being depleted too much in down markets. The severe market declines in 1973–74 caused the S&P 500 to fall much further than the other two investments. The continued income withdrawals during such severe down periods makes it very difficult for the account to rebound once the markets recover.

Perhaps the most important message contained in this comparison is that income investors should not assume that a fixed investment vehicle is necessary to provide a dependable income. They should focus on total returns from their investments. Income investors must use Asset Class Investing with lower variances than pure equity accounts when they seek higher total rates of return. Increased total returns will give them the cash flow necessary to meet their retirement needs and keep pace with inflation if they've minimized risk through diversification. Asset Class Investing provides a prudent solution to this retirement dilemma.

The goal of your retirement account should be to combine optimally various asset classes to give the highest possible returns at the level of risk with which you are comfortable. This focus on risk and the reduction of variance in your account value lets you accumulate wealth steadily while maintaining peace of mind. High, risk-adjusted rates of return and a dependable income stream are the goals of many investors. Asset Class Investing provides academically sound solutions and a means to reach these goals.

To make all this work, you need the right tools. In the next chapter, we'll explore the building blocks of Asset Class Investing, and the tools that you need to reach your financial goals.

ENDNOTES

[1]Markowitz, Harry, *The Journal of Finance* 7, no. 1 (March 1952), pp. 77-91.

[2]Ellis, Charles D., *Investment Policy* (New York: Dow Jones Irwin, 1985).

[3]Sharpe, William F., "Are Gains Likely From Market Timing?" *Financial Analysts Journal* (March–April 1975), as adapted in *The Asset Allocation Decision*, SEI Research Report (SEI Capital Resources, April 1992).

[4]"Active versus Passive Investing," *The Journal of Investing* 2, no. 1 (Spring 1993).

[5]Jeffrey, Robert H., "The Folly of Stock Market Timing," *Harvard Business Review* (July–August 1984).

[6]Brinson, Gary P.; L. Randolph Hood; and Gilbert L. Beebower, *Financial Analysts Journal* (July–August 1986), pp. 39–44.

Chapter Six

Institutional Asset Class Funds–The New Paradigm

I t is now clear that in building your portfolio, you must use investments that have dissimilar price movements. In this chapter, we will
show you the most effective tool for accomplishing this diversification:
the institutional asset class mutual fund, our third key concept in Asset
Class Investing.

Initially, these types of mutual funds were not available to the public.
Often their minimum required investment was in the millions of dollars,
effectively removing them from the retail marketplace. When we first started
offering our investment strategies to our clients, we were forced to use the
retail mutual funds available to the general public. We found significant
structural problems with these funds. We didn't have any choices when we
first got started. But along the way we discovered better tools. You will, too.

INSTITUTIONAL ASSET CLASS MUTUAL FUNDS

Institutional asset class mutual funds are mutual funds that represent
entire market segments of securities with similar risk characteristics.
They can be used as tools to achieve effective dissimilar-price-movement diversification. In the past, they have only been available to large,
institutional investors.

The four major attributes of institutional asset class mutual funds are
listed below.

1. Lower operating expenses

2. Lower turnover, resulting in lower taxes

3. Lower trading costs

4. Consistently maintained market segments

We will discuss each attribute in turn.

Lower Operating Expenses

Institutional asset class mutual funds are true no-load mutual funds. A true no-load mutual fund has no sales commissions when you purchase or redeem shares. It has no back-end loads, redemption fees, or 12b–1 marketing fees. However, all mutual funds have operating expenses, which include management fees and administrative expenses. The average retail equity mutual fund today has a total expense ratio of 1.45 percent.[1] The expense ratio is the operating expenses, expressed as a percentage of average net assets. Operating expenses include management, administrative, and custody fees. The operating expenses of the average retail mutual fund are almost three times greater than those for funds available to institutions. It's the difference between buying retail and buying wholesale. Other factors being equal, lower costs lead to higher rates of return over time.

An important study by Elton, Gruber, et al., found that not only did retail equity mutual funds underperform the market, but the managers with the highest operating expenses had the worst performance.[2] The results of this study, illustrated in Table 6–1, show that, in general, the higher the expense ratio, the lower the performance. It seems the more mediocre the performance, the higher the fee.

TABLE 6–1
Relation of Alphas and Expense Ratios

Mutual Fund's Range of Operating Expenses (E) %				%	Excess Return Over Market α
0.91	<	E	<	2.02	-3.87
0.75	<	E	<	0.91	-1.68
0.68	<	E	<	0.75	-0.69
0.59	<	E	<	0.68	-1.19
		E	<	0.59	-0.59

If mutual fund managers outperformed the market as a whole, they have a positive alpha (α). Alpha measures excess returns over market returns.[3] The more positive the alpha, the more the manager outperformed the market. In Table 6–1, all the alphas in the aggregate were negative for each range of operating expenses. This means that managers, on average, were underperforming the market by an amount greater than their operating expenses. Table 6–1 shows that the worst performers were the mutual funds that charged the most. This was one of the reasons we looked into institutional asset class mutual funds.

Lower Turnover, Lower Taxes

The average retail mutual fund had an approximately 75 percent turnover in 1994.[4] This indicates that 75 percent of the mutual fund's assets were traded in 1994. If you had invested $100,000, approximately $75,000 worth of the underlying securities would have been bought and sold during the year. This is important because each time you trade, there is a transaction cost involved—whether it's a commission and/or the "bid/ask" spread—that can easily amount to much more than the total operating expenses disclosed in the fund's prospectus.

Why do retail mutual funds have such high turnover? First, as we've already stated, fund managers are under tremendous pressure to perform. Second, the only way that a mutual fund manager can add value that is "perceived in the market" is to attempt to guess at market turning points or the individual securities that are going to outperform the market. Just attempting these two feats creates substantial turnover. By the laws of probability, a few of them will succeed, but most will not. Third, a portion of the retail public is chasing performance. They tend to move in and out of retail mutual funds, forcing managers to buy and sell more often than they would like.

What happens when mutual fund managers succeed? They are highlighted in the financial press and money comes racing in. Imagine that you are a mutual fund manager and you were just written up in *The Wall Street Journal* as manager of the top-performing mutual fund for the year. Not only are your parents proud, but you are likely to receive a significant increase in new investments immediately from the public. They want to participate in your newfound success. Who pays the cost of investing these funds? The existing shareholders bear the burden of investing new money, not the new investors. If you have a mutual fund with $500 million now, and $100 million comes in, that's a 20 percent increase in assets. The new shareholders are going to buy at today's net asset prices (NAV). You, the fund manager, now have to buy securities for your new investors with their $100 million. The tradings costs of investing that amount of money will be significant. You may have some market impact and drive up the prices of the very stock you are buying with this additional $100 million. The market impact would likely be very significant if your mutual fund, for example, invests in small company stocks.

So, if you are an existing investor and take a long-term perspective and stay in a fund that has "hot money" coming in, you're going to bear the cost. What happens when the performance is poor? Well, the fund may be featured again on page one of *The Wall Street Journal*. The active mutual fund manager's parents are no longer proud. And $100 million or more leaves the fund—who pays that cost? The exiting shareholders are able to redeem at NAV, so the cost of selling out that portfolio is also borne by the existing shareholders. Institutional investors won't put up with it, so they will not invest in publicly available funds. That's why they've created this separation between themselves and the public. You should, too.

Elton, Gruber, et al., also studied turnover among mutual funds.[5] Not surprisingly, as Table 6–2 shows, the greater the turnover, the more negative the alpha. As investors, we want mutual funds that we invest in to have positive alphas. If not, we can simply invest in an index mutual fund for that market segment and have an implied alpha of zero—much better than all these negative alphas we keep seeing.

TABLE 6–2
Relation of Turnover and Alphas

%	Mutual Fund's Range of Turnover (T)			%	Excess Return Over Market α
72	<	T	<	168	-2.21
51	<	T	<	72	-1.87
34	<	T	<	51	-2.17
22	<	T	<	34	-1.11
		T	<	22	-0.58

You can have control over the first two attributes, operating expenses and turnover, by selecting the right mutual funds. We noticed that institutional investors significantly increased their returns through lowered costs and turnover after demanding a separate group of mutual funds for institutions. Individuals can now get access to these funds.

But access solves only half the problem. Our clients, unlike most institutions, are subject to taxes. We have to determine how effective institutional asset class mutual funds would be in a taxable environment.

Each time the mutual fund manager sells a security, assuming that you have a profit, you realize a capital gain. Mutual funds are required to distribute 98 percent of their taxable income each year, including realized capital gains, to stay tax-exempt at the mutual fund level. Since no mutual fund manager wants to have his or her performance reduced by paying corporate income taxes, the funds distribute all income. You will receive dividends for both ordinary income, made up of interest and stock dividends, and capital-gain distributions from profitable sales made by your mutual fund. If your mutual fund has a turnover of 80 percent per year, on average you will realize 80 percent of the capital gains and these will be taxable each year. On the other hand, if you use institutional asset class funds, the average turnover is approximately 16 percent—84 percent of the taxable gains are deferred until you want to recognize them.

Two recent academic studies indicate that mutual fund capital gains and dividends reduce after-tax returns for shareholders, and that asset class mutual funds can protect against those tax losses. These two studies, one from Stanford University and the other published in the *Journal of Portfolio Management*, demonstrate that tax efficiency is an important factor to consider in equity mutual fund selection. Numerous mutual funds, in their quest for top performance, reduce their shareholders' potential after-tax returns by producing high taxable distributions, including capital gains resulting from frequent buying and selling of appreciated securities in a fund. Dividends, taxed as ordinary income, may also reduce potential after-tax returns.

In a study commissioned by Charles Schwab & Company, Inc. and conducted by John B. Shoven, Professor of Economics at Stanford University, and Joel M. Dickson, a Stanford Ph.D. candidate, taxable distributions were found to have an impact on the rates of return of many well-known retail equity mutual funds.[6] The study measured the performance of 62 equity funds for the 30-year period from 1963 through the end of 1992. It found that the high-tax investor who reinvested only after-tax distributions would end up with accumulated wealth, per dollar invested, equal to less than half (45 percent) of the funds' published performances. An investor in the middle tax bracket would see only 55 percent of the performance published by the funds.

Another study, by Robert H. Jeffrey and Robert D. Arnott, published in the *Journal of Portfolio Management,* concluded that extremely low portfolio turnover can be a factor in improving a fund's potential after-tax performance.[7] Asset class funds typically have very low portfolio turnover, which translates into less frequent trading and therefore may result in a lower capital gains. Low turnover may also benefit share-holders by holding down trading costs.

Jeffrey and Arnott compared the performances of large, actively managed equity mutual funds and a passively managed equity index fund from 1982 to 1991. They found that only 21 percent (15 of the 72 equity funds) outperformed the index fund on a pretax basis during that period. Only 5 of the 72 funds outperformed the index fund after fac-toring in taxes. The Jeffrey and Arnott study raises the important point that despite high turnover and capital-gain distributions, some funds can produce higher after-tax returns than others with low portfolio turnover and no capital-gain distributions. This was demonstrated by the five funds in the Jeffrey study that outpaced the after-tax returns of an index fund over the nine years examined. Jeffrey and Arnott note, however, that it may be difficult to predict which funds will exhibit that performance. "While it is tempting to assume that these exceptions are evidence that 'it can be done' (i.e., that funds producing superior after–tax returns can be identified 10 years in advance), the reality is that the chances of success are slim at best."

The Jeffrey and Arnott study concluded that "passive indexing is a very difficult strategy to beat on an after-tax basis and, therefore, active taxable strategies should always be benchmarked against the after-tax performance of an indexed alternative."

Another tax problem associated with most mutual funds can be seen in the stock market crash of October 19, 1987. After the crash, most mutual fund managers decided that they would "clean house," which led to higher-than-normal portfolio turnover rates for that year. The higher turnover rates yielded very large capital-gain distributions. Many stocks that had appreciated during the bull market preceding the crash were sold. The result for most investors was the forced recognition of large amounts of capital gains passed on to them by the fund. For exam-ple, if you had invested $10,000 in Fidelity Magellan mutual fund on December 31, 1986, you would have shown a loss of 8.3 percent in your account as of December 31, 1987. Although you would have been dis-appointed to have a loss for the year (through the depreciation of the net asset value), the real shock would have come on April 15, 1988, when, as a 28 percent tax bracket investor, you would have paid $566 in capital gains taxes generated by the sale of some stocks that still had profits to take.

This example describes the fate of many investors who were forced to pay taxes on their mutual funds even though their accounts were down for the year. It is frustrating to have your mutual funds decline in value, yet have to pay taxes on "phantom" gains.

Lower Trading Costs

Trading costs can be much more significant than operating expenses and harder to determine. Let's just examine one trade that a mutual fund might execute over the counter, through NASDAQ. If the stock was currently at $10 ask and $9.50 bid, what would be the cost of buying and selling the stock, assuming no price change? You'd buy a stock at the ask price of $10 and sell it at the bid price of $9.50—a $0.50 loss. This loss is what the market maker earns for facilitating the trade. This represents a 5 percent cost of trading on your purchase price of $10. If your portfolio turned over 80 percent during the year, you would have a cost of 80 percent of 5 percent, or a total hidden cost due to turnover of 4 percent—a hidden cost that can derail your investment program.

Trading costs can far exceed management fees. Trading costs are made up of agency costs (commissions and/or the bid/ask spread) and market impact. While trading costs are greater for small company stocks than for large company stocks, they are very significant for both.

Trading costs increase significantly as you invest in smaller company stocks. To calculate this effect, we need to define a range of sizes. We start with the New York Stock Exchange (NYSE). As of the end of 1993, there were 2,290 companies on the NYSE. In Table 6–3, we have divided those companies into 10 equal groups (deciles) based on market size. Market size is based on market capitalization, which is equal to the market price of that issue multiplied by the number of shares outstanding. Each NYSE decile holds 229 stocks, ranked by market size. We have included American Stock Exchange (AMEX) and NASDAQ issues in the last two columns, allocated by their market size.

General Electric Company was the largest corporation listed on the NYSE and had a market capitalization of over $89 billion on December 31, 1993.

TABLE 6–3
Market Capitalization

Market Capitalization Decile	Size ($M)	Largest Co. in Decile (NYSE)	Number of Companies NYSE	AMEX	NASDAQ
1	89,452	General Electric Co.	229	5	24
2	5,060	Upjohn Co.	229	4	37
3	2,242	First of America Bank Corp.	229	13	60
4	1,215	Boston Scientific Co.	229	18	100
5	718	Tektronix Inc.	229	19	131
6	464	Carpenter Technology	229	25	172
7	302	Parker Drilling Co.	229	30	252
8	196	Commercial Intertech	229	54	329
9	125	Giant Inds Inc.	229	112	583
10	68	Ampco-Pittsburgh Corp.	229	546	1,466

Size is defined by NYSE market capitalization deciles.
Market capitalization = price x shares outstanding. Data as of December 31, 1993.

The largest company in the 10th decile was Ampco–Pittsburgh Corp., with a market size of only $68 million. What a difference! These differences in size play a significant factor in trading costs. The smaller the market size, the higher the potential trading costs and the smaller the daily trading volume.

TABLE 6–4
Bid-Ask Spread

Size Decile	Average Price $	Percent Spread %	Daily Trading Volume per Issue Shares	Dollars ($)
1	$52.35	0.46	619,163	29,368,443
2	42.03	0.69	279,342	9,905,924
3	31.35	0.85	215,013	5,808,295
4	29.89	1.19	129,293	3,188,392
5	24.77	1.33	104,839	1,931,157
6	21.83	1.73	73,492	1,295,661
7	20.24	2.10	49,876	812,266
8	17.22	2.58	46,409	657,260
9	14.13	3.53	24,877	282,201
10	8.41	6.82	11,315	70,220

Source: *PC Quote* (January 11, 1994).

The bid/ask spread as a percentage of price is a conservative estimate of actual trading costs. This estimate is over 14 times greater for the smallest decile than for the largest decile (6.82 vs. 0.46 percent). An investor purchasing at the ask price and selling at the bid price would pay trading costs of 0.46 percent for the largest stocks and 6.82 percent for the smallest stocks (if the trades do not move the market). A large order that is a significant part of the daily trading volume is likely to move the market against the investor, adding an additional cost. Twenty-nine million dollars represents the daily trading volume of a single stock in decile 1, or more than the combined volume of 400 stocks in decile 10 (see Table 6–4). In Chapter Seven, we will see that trading costs are even higher when you invest internationally.

As a rule of thumb, an investor can calculate a very conservative trading cost estimate by multiplying a mutual fund's turnover ratio by the bid/ask percentage spread for its average market capitalization. For example, a mutual fund with an average market capitalization in the 5th decile, with a turnover of 203 percent, would have estimated hidden costs of trading, calculated at: 2.03 x 1.33% = 2.69%.

Consistently Maintained Market Segments

Most investment advisors now agree that the largest determinant of performance is asset allocation. And effective asset allocation can only be accomplished if the building blocks you use maintain consistent market segments. If you are using traditional retail mutual funds, the manager may change its exposure over time, significantly changing the effectiveness of your allocation.

In Figures 6–1 and 6–2, we have utilized Ibbotson & Associates' Attribution software to compare two popular funds, Fidelity Magellan and Vanguard Index 500 (S&P 500) from January 1983 through December 1994. In examining the exposure distributions, it becomes very apparent that the portion of Fidelity Magellan's return that is explained by the corresponding benchmark return over time changed dramatically when contrasted with the Vanguard Index 500. In January 1983, the exposure was as follows: Wilshire Small Growth, 84 percent; Wilshire Large Value, 10 percent; and Long-Term Government bonds, 6 percent. By December 1994, the exposure had changed to Wilshire Large Value, 40 percent; Wilshire Large Growth, 12 percent; Wilshire MidCap Value, 22 percent; EAFE (excluding Japan), 10 percent; Japan, 3 percent; and Wilshire Small Growth, 11 percent.

FIGURE 6–1
Fidelity Magellan

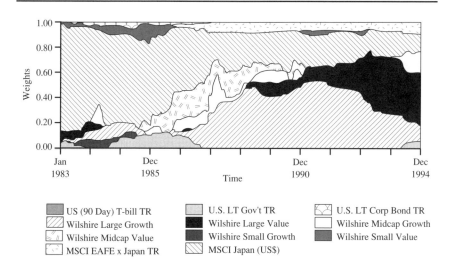

FIGURE 6–2
Vanguard Index 500

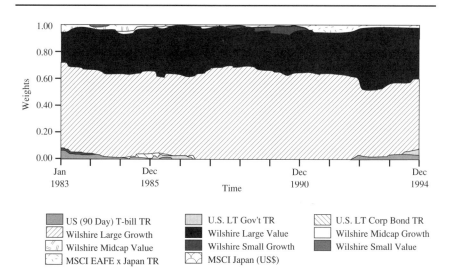

TABLE 6–5
Asset Class Mutual Funds Available to the Public

Fund Name	Investment Objective	Fund Inception Date	Fund Family	Phone
Ambassador Indexed Stock Ret A	Growth-Inc	12/92	Ambassador Funds	800-892-4366
American Gas Index	Sp. Nat. Res.	5/89	Rushman Group	800-343-3355
ASM	Growth-Inc.	3/91	ASM Fund	800-445-2763
Benham Global Natural Res Index	Sp. Nat. Res.	9/94	Benham Group	800-331-8331
Benham Gold Equities Index	Sp. Metals	8/88	Benham Group	800-331-8331
Biltmore Equity Index	Growth-Inc	5/93	Biltmore Funds	800-462-7538
BT Investment Equity 500 Index	Growth	12/92	BT Funds	800-943-2222
California Investment S&P 500 Index	Growth-Inc	4/92	California Investment Trust Group	800-328-7408
California Investment S&P MidCap	Growth-Inc	4/92	California Investment Trust Group	800-225-8778
Capital Market Index	Growth-Inc	11/92	Capital Market Fund	800-328-7408
Composite Northwest 50A	Growth	11/86	Composite Group of Funds	800-543-8072
Composite Northwest 50B	Growth	3/94	Composite Group of Funds	800-543-8072
Dean Witter Value- Add Market Equity	Growth Inc	12/87	Dean Witter Funds	800-869-3863
Domini Social Equity	Growth-Inc	6/91	Domini Social Equity Trust	800-762-6814
Dreyfus Edison Electric	Sp. Util	12/91	Dreyfus Group	800-645-6561
Dreyfus-Wilshire Lrg Co Grth	Growth	10/92	Dreyfus Group	800-645-6561
Dreyfus-Wilshire Lrg Co Val	Growth	10/92	Dreyfus Group	800-645-6561
Dreyfus-Wilshire Sm Co Grth	Small Company	10/92	Dreyfus Group	800-645-6561
Dreyfus-Wilshire Sm Co Value	Small Company	10/92	Dreyfus Group	800-645-6561
Fidelity Market Index	Growth-Inc	3/90	Fidelity Group	800-544-8888
First American Equity Index A	Growth-Inc	8/94	First American Investment Funds	800-637-2548
First American Equity Index B	Growth-Inc	12/92	First American Investment Funds	800-637-2548
Galaxy II Large Co Index Ret	Growth-Inc	10/90	Galaxy Funds	800-628-0414
Galaxy II Small Co Index Ret	Small Company	10/90	Galaxy Funds	800-628-0414
Galaxy II U.S.. Treasury Index Ret	Gvt Treasury	6/91	Galaxy Funds	800-628-0414
Galaxy II Utility Index Ret	Sp. Util	1/93	Galaxy Funds	800-628-0414
Gateway Index Plus	Growth-Inc	12/77	Gateway Group	800-345-6339
Gateway Mid-Cap Index	Growth	9/92	Gateway Group	800-354-6339
Gateway Small Cap Index	Small Company	6/93	Gateway Group	800-354-6339
Goldman Sachs Core F/I Instl	Corp General	1/94	Goldman Sachs Asset Management Group	800-621-2550
Jackson National Growth	Growth	11/92	Jackson National Capital Management Funds	800-888-3863
Kent Index Equity Investment	Growth-In	12/92	Kent Funds	800-633-5368
MainStay Equity Index	Growth-In	12/90	MainStay Funds	800-522-4202
Monitrend Summation	Growth-Inc	2/88	Monitrend Mutual Funds	800-251-1970

TABLE 6–5 (*continued*)

Fund Name	Investment Objective	Fund Inception Date	Fund Family	Phone
Nations Equity- Index Tr A	Growth	12/93	Nations Funds	800-321-7854
Peoples Index	Growth-Inc	1/90	Dreyfus Group	800-645-6561
Peoples S&P MidCap Index	Growth	6/91	Dreyfus Group	800-645-6561
PNC Index Equity Inv	Growth-Inc	6/92	PNC Family of Funds	800-422-6538
Portico Bond Immdex	Corp Hi Qlty	12/89	Portico Funds	800-228-1024
Portico Equity Index	Growth-Inc	12/89	Portico Funds	800-228-1024
Pricipal Pres S&P 100 Plus	Growth-Inc	12/85	Principal Preservation Portfolios	800-826-4600
Schwab 1000	Growth-Inc	4/91	Schwab Funds	800-526-8600
Schwab International Index	Foreign	9/93	Schwab Funds	800-526-8600
Schwab Small Cap Index	Small Company	12/93	Schwab Funds	800-526-8600
Seven Seas Matrix Equity	Growth	5/92	Seven Seas Series Fund	800-647-7327
Seven Seas S&P 500 Index	Growth-Inc	12/92	Seven Seas Series Fund	800-647-7327
Seven Seas Small Cap	Small Company	7/92	Seven Seas Series Fund	800-647-7327
Smith Breeden Mkt Tracking	Growth-Inc	6/92	Smith Breeden Family of Funds	800-221-3138
Stagecoach Corporate Stock	Growth-Inc	1/84	Stagecoach Funds	800-222-8222
STI Classic Intl Equity Index Inv	Foreign	6/94	STI Classic Funds	800-428-6970
T. Rowe Price Equity Index	Growth-Inc	3/90	Price T. Rowe Funds	800-638-5660
United Svcs All American Equity	Growth-Inc	3/81	United Services Funds	800-873-8637
Vanguard Balanced Index	Balanced	9/92	Vanguard Group	800-662-7447
Vanguard Bond Index Int-Term	Corp General	3/94	Vanguard Group	800-662-7447
Vanguard Bond Index Long-Term	Corp General	3/94	Vanguard Group	800-662-7447
Vanguard Bond Index Short-Term	Corp General	3/94	Vanguard Group	800-662-7447
Vanguard Bond Index Total Bd	Corp Hi Qlty	12/86	Vanguard Group	800-662-7447
Vanguard Index 500	Growth-Inc	8/76	Vanguard Group	800-662-7447
Vanguard Index Extended Market	Small Company	12/87	Vanguard Group	800-662-7447
Vanguard Index Growth	Growth	11/92	Vanguard Group	800-662-7447
Vanguard Index Small Cap Stock	Small Company	10/60	Vanguard Group	800-662-7447
Vanguard Index Total Stk Mkt	Growth-Inc	4/92	Vanguard Group	800-662-7447
Vanguard Index Value	Growth-Inc	11/92	Vanguard Group	800-662-7447
Vanguard International Equity Emerg Mkt	Foreign	3/94	Vanguard Group	800-662-7447
Vanguard International Equity European	Europe	6/90	Vanguard Group	800-662-7447
Vanguard International Equity Pacific	Pacific	6/90	Vanguard Group	800-662-7447
Vanguard Quantitative	Growth-Inc	12/86	Vanguard Group	800-662-7447
Victory Stock Index	Growth-Inc	12/93	Victory Group	800-539-3863
Woodward Equity Index Ret	Growth-Inc	7/92	Woodward Funds	800-688-3350

Source: Morningstar Inc., All rights reserved.

This significant change in exposure, as contrasted with the modest change in the Vanguard Fund, would make Fidelity Magellan's inclusion in an asset allocation difficult at best, if you were trying to control the asset allocation. If you want to maintain a consistent allocation, then only mutual funds that may have relatively constant exposures should be considered. Institutional asset class funds are, by their very design, consistent in their exposures.

Unfortunately, the retail investor has not been adequately exposed to Asset Class Investing—until now. Without this exposure, there has been little demand for making institutional asset class mutual funds available to the public. With management fees averaging only one-third the cost of retail funds, it is unlikely that many mutual fund sponsors will be enlightening the public.

Asset Class Mutual Funds Currently Available

To date, there are several progressive mutual fund families offering retail asset class mutual funds to the public (See Table 6–5).[8] These funds are very similar to the institutional asset class funds, but still face many of the inherent problems of being available to the retail public. For investors with portfolios of less than $100,000, though, they can add substantial value over traditional retail mutual funds.

THE NEW INVESTMENT PROFESSIONAL

In Chapter Fourteen, we will show you how to build your own portfolio using these retail asset class mutual funds. It is a good place to get started if you have less than $100,000 to invest. However, as we discussed earlier, these retail asset class mutual funds are still subject to many of the problems that retail mutual funds in general experience.

To better serve our clients, we knew we wanted to avoid the retail mutual funds and gain access for our clients to the institutional mutual funds. We accomplished this by forming strategic alliances with the major institutional asset class providers. These providers normally work directly with clients, typically large pension plans worth a billion dollars or more. With only a few people in customer support (the typical retail mutual funds may have over 500 just answering the phones), they were not equipped to work with the public. In addition, their institutional clients did not want them to make their mutual funds available to the public if they were not investing strategically for the long term. We were committed to educating our clients about how investments work and to designing an investment program with institutional asset class funds that would allow them not to fall prey to the normal retail concerns. Our firm was one of the first to incorporate these strategic alliances to gain access to these funds for its clients. As the industry has taken note, new alliances have developed, leading to the emergence of a new investment professional: the institutional asset class mutual fund advisor. In Chapter Fourteen, we will show you how to select an institutional asset class mutual fund advisor.

WHICH ASSET CLASSES DO YOU USE?

Now that you have access to asset class mutual funds, which ones should you utilize? To start, examine the historical performance of each investment category. This will allow you to get a better understanding of how each asset class has performed over a long period of time. This is not to say that the past indicates future performance; however, it does indicate reasonable relationships between various asset classes.

FIGURE 6–3
Stocks, Bonds, Bills, and Inflation, January 1926 to December 1994

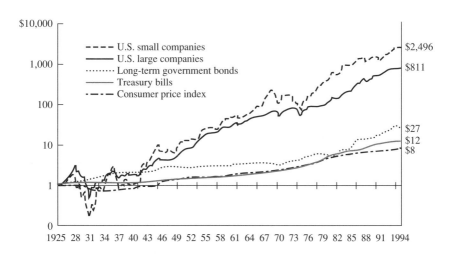

Time series information on domestic asset classes is readily available for you to review, starting with 1926. This time period includes the Great Depression, World War II, the Korean War, the Vietnam War, and numerous other major world crises. How did the investment markets perform? In Figure 6–3, you can see that, historically, equities have far outperformed fixed-income asset classes. If you had invested $1 in the S&P 500 index at the beginning of 1926, it would have been worth $811 (assuming reinvestment of dividends) by the end of 1994, while a $1 investment in small company stocks would have been worth almost $2,500.

Fixed-income asset classes had trouble keeping pace with inflation. That same dollar invested in 20-year U.S. government bonds would have been worth $27, and $12 if you had invested in 30-day U.S. Treasury bills. Investments over this period required an increase in value of $8 simply to maintain purchasing power. The inflation rate is the absolute minimum goal for most investors. Many investors need to do significantly better to provide for their tax liabilities and their families' quality of life.

Table 6–6 illustrates that not only have equities outperformed fixed-income asset classes, they also easily outpaced inflation. Table 6–6 shows a series of time periods. Over each of the periods, the S&P 500 index increased more than both long-term U.S. government bonds and inflation. In most periods, the long-term U.S. government bond market barely exceeded inflation. Even in the years during which government bonds substantially beat the inflation rate, the S&P 500 beat both.

TABLE 6–6
Nominal Annualized Total Returns

Number of Years	Time Period	S&P 500 %	Govt. Bonds %	Inflation (CPI) %
68	1926–94	10.2	04.8	3.1
50	1945–94	11.9	05.0	4.4
40	1955–94	10.7	05.6	4.4
30	1965–94	10.0	07.0	5.4
20	1975–94	14.6	09.5	5.5
10	1985–94	14.4	12.0	3.6
5	1990–94	08.7	08.6	3.5

Table 6–7 looks at the inflation-adjusted ("real") returns of 15-year time periods. Stocks dominated bonds in all periods. This time, however, both U.S. government and corporate issues are examined. In each period,

equities beat fixed-income assets by varying degrees. Interestingly, even in the period ending in 1980, when all three assets had negative returns after adjusting for inflation, the equities lost the least. In fact, the stock market, which has often been stereotyped as too risky, ironically had only one negative 15-year period, while Treasuries and corporate bonds each had two.

TABLE 6–7
Real (Inflation-Adjusted) Annualized Returns

Asset Class	1980 –94 %	1979 –93 %	1978 –92 %	1977 –91 %	1976 –90 %	1966 –80 %	1956 –70 %	1946 –60 %
S&P 500 index	9.8	10.3	9.6	8.2	7.7	-0.5	5.6	10.1
Long-term corporate bonds	6.5	5.9	4.9	3.7	3.6	-3.9	0.6	-1.9
30-day Treasury bills	2.9	2.6	2.5	2.4	2.2	-0.6	1.0	-2.0

THE TIME HORIZON

Modern Portfolio Theory states that investments in equities will produce higher expected returns than investments in fixed-income assets, given the higher risks inherent in equity markets. These risks are due primarily to the cyclical swings of the stock market. These cyclical swings are of greatest concern to those investors who plan to liquidate their investments in the near future. In light of most investors' long-term perspectives, it is prudent to attempt to achieve a higher rate of return by investing a large portion of your portfolio's assets in equities.

The minimum time horizon for you to invest in equities should be no less than five years. For any portfolio with less than a five-year horizon, the portfolio should be predominantly made up of fixed-income investments. This five-year minimum investment period is critical. The investment process must be viewed as a long-term plan for achieving the desired results. This is because the one-year volatility can be significant for certain asset classes. However, the range of probable returns over a five-year period is greatly reduced.

Some portion of the portfolio's assets may be invested in fixed-income investments to help reduce the overall level of risk in the portfolio. Fixed-income investments tend to be less volatile than equities. Fixed instruments should be used to reduce the overall level of risk to your comfort level.

FIXED-INCOME ASSET CLASSES

Many investors purchase bonds and bond mutual funds as part of a comprehensive investment portfolio. Long-term vehicles, such as U.S. Treasury bonds, are thought to be attractive because of their safety and higher yields. They are considered "safe" due to the high credit quality of these bonds, which are backed by the full faith and credit of the U.S. government.

A bond represents a loan to the issuer, such as the U.S. government, usually in return for periodic, fixed-interest payments. These payments continue until the bond is redeemed at maturity (or earlier if called by the issuer). At the time of maturity, the face value of the bond is returned to the investor. Bonds with maturities of less than 5 years are considered short-term bonds; those with maturities between 5 and 12 years are inter-mediate-term bonds; and bonds with maturities longer than 12 years are long-term bonds.

The major risk you face in bonds is interest rate risk. Prices of bonds move in the opposite direction of interest rates; thus, when interest rates rise, prices of bonds fall—and vice versa. For example, consider a newly issued 20-year Treasury bond with a 6 percent coupon rate purchased 12 months ago. If, in the last year, interest rates had increased by 2 percent, new 20-year Treasury bonds would be offered with 8 percent coupons. The 6 percent bonds would be worth less than the newly issued 8 percent bonds, due to the former's lower coupon rate. This illustrates how falling interest rates force bond prices up. Alternatively, interest rates may fall and force bond prices up. The inverse relationship between interest rates and bond values is a risk that you must evaluate.

Figure 6–4 illustrates the historical rates of total returns for 20-year Treasury bonds over six decades. During the 1980s, long-term-bond investors enjoyed their best decade in history, with gains averaging 12.7 percent per year. Unfortunately, many investors only consider the most recent period when analyzing their investment options. Psychologists call this *cognition bias*. We call it "rear-view-mirror investment." It is like try-ing to drive a car while only looking at where you have been through the rear-view mirror. It is critical to analyze all statistical evidence available in financial decision making. You never want to dismiss data without a very good reason.

Consider the 1950s. It was the worst decade for long-term-bond investors, with an average annual loss of -0.1 percent if you reinvested the interest income, and a substantially greater loss if you did not. This practical example of the interest rate risk of long-term bonds illustrates what can happen when interest rates rise. The volatility of long-term bonds, particularly over long time periods, approaches the volatility of common stocks. Clearly, long-term U.S. Treasury bonds don't have the price stability that many fixed-income investors are seeking.

FIGURE 6–4
Long-Term Treasury Bond Returns through Six Decades

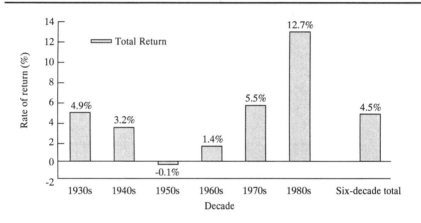

When the marketplace values a bond, the length of time to maturity is critically important. The longer the time to maturity, the longer the expected stream of interest payments to the bond holder. The market price of any bond represents the present value of this stream of interest payments, discounted at the currently offered interest rates. As interest rates fluctuate, the present value of this stream of interest payments constantly changes. A longer stream of interest payments, which long-term bonds have versus short-term bonds, creates higher price volatility.

The higher risk of long-term bonds is acceptable, provided we are sufficiently compensated with higher rates of return for the additional risk. Eugene Fama has studied the rates of return for long-term bonds from 1964 to 1990.[9] His research shows that long-term bonds historically have had wide variances in their rates of total return without sufficiently compensating investors with higher expected returns. He found that bonds with maturities beyond five years actually have had lower total returns and higher standard deviations than those with maturities of less than five years.

The predominant investors in the long-term bond markets are institutions, including corporate pension plans and life insurance companies. These investors are interested in funding long-term debt obligations such as fixed annuity payments or other fixed corporate responsibilities. They are not concerned with volatility of principal, nor with the effects of inflation, since their obligations are fixed amounts. You, however, are concerned with inflation and volatility. You live in a variable-rate world and have a limited tolerance for volatility.

In terms of variability of total returns, long-term bonds look more like stocks than like shorter-term, fixed-income vehicles such as Treasury bills. And yet, over long time periods, the respective total returns of long-term bonds and Treasury bills have consistently lagged those of equities. Figure 6–5 illustrates the higher standard deviations and lower total returns of bonds with maturities beyond five years.

Your purpose in holding some fixed-income asset classes should be to lower the risk of the overall portfolio. Replacing the traditional long-term bonds with a combination of common stocks and short-term, fixed-income vehicles will maintain the portfolio's expected rate of return while decreasing its volatility.

Studies show that the efficient-market hypothesis holds true not only for stocks, as we discussed in Chapter Three, but for the bond market as well. There is no ability to predict future changes in interest rates. Interest rate changes, as well as equity price changes, are immediately priced into the market. The best estimate of the future price of any fixed instrument is the price of a similar instrument today. There appear to be, on average, no money managers who are able to predict interest rate movements in an attempt to provide superior returns.

In building your portfolio, you need to recognize the role fixed investments play. The fixed investments are in your asset class portfolio simply to mitigate risk. For that reason, it makes no sense to have longer maturity instruments, unless you have a specific time-horizon liability and you will be funding it with a matching debt instrument. The risk inherent in the greater volatility of long-term bonds, without the reward for that risk, results in our recommendation that you avoid all debt instruments with maturities beyond five years. In addition, to maintain a high-quality portfolio, we recommend that you hold only government or high-quality debt instruments of AAA rating.

Institutional asset class funds attempt to add value without predicting future changes in the market. In the case of a bond fund, there will be no interest rate forecasting beyond the implicit forecast of the yield curve. However, alternative strategies still can be used to enhance returns. Research concludes that the current yield curve is the best estimate of future yield curves.[10] This estimate enables asset class mutual fund managers to calculate the expected returns and determine optimal maturity and holding periods.

FIGURE 6–5
Risk and Reward for Bonds, 1964–94

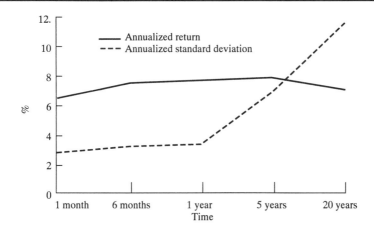

The current shape of the yield curve will determine the choice of maturity. In Figure 6–6, the fixed-income institutional asset class mutual fund has the constraints of a maximum maturity of two years and a maximum average maturity of one year. The manager will extend maturities within these constraints when there is an anticipated reward for doing so. This will occur when the yield curve is steep.

The money manager will stay with short maturities in his selection of debt instruments when longer maturities do not provide additional returns. With an inverted yield curve, as illustrated in Figure 6–7, the money manager will invest in cash equivalents.

Using the current yield curve as an estimate of future yield curves, the money manager can construct a matrix of expected returns, which can then be used to determine the optimal maturity and holding period. In Figure 6–8 the highest expected annualized return is 9.73 percent for a strategy of buying a fixed instrument with a maturity of 18 months and selling it 3 months later, when time to maturity is 15 months.

FIGURE 6–6
Determining Optimal Maturities: Yield Curve 1

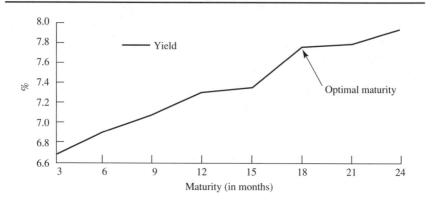

FIGURE 6–7
Determining Optimal Maturities: Yield Curve 2

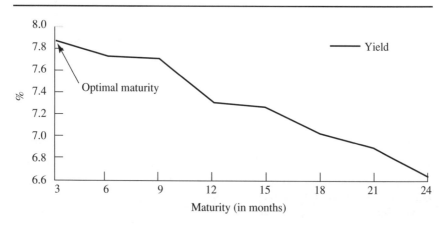

This investment strategy is known as the matrix pricing strategy. It has been developed by leading theoreticians in finance and is the basis of several investment funds. It is simply riding the yield curve. In studies as well as applications, it appears to add 50–100 basis points over comparable index funds annually over extended periods of time. *For our clients, we currently utilize three fixed-income asset classes: a money market; a one-year, high-quality corporate bond; and a five-year government-bond mutual fund.*

FIGURE 6–8
Finding the Optimal Maturity and Holding Period

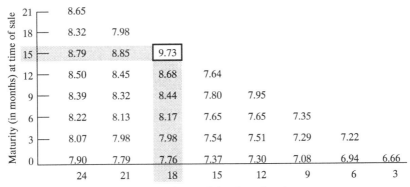

TAX-FREE SECURITIES AS AN ASSET CLASS

You may question why we did not mention tax-free securities in the recommended fixed-income portion of your asset class portfolio. All things being equal, most individual investors would prefer to have tax-free rather than taxable income. But all things are not equal. Let's examine how the taxable fixed-income market works and then contrast it with the tax-exempt market. Most people who invest in fixed-income asset classes are attracted by the steady income and minimal risk. However, due to the extreme volatility of interest rates since the mid-1970s, fixed-income investors have been subject to increasing risk. As interest rates have risen, the market value of those investments has fallen due to the lower yield. Investors have preferred the new bonds that have higher interest rates. In a rising interest rate market, you have to resign yourself to either accepting the lower interest rate of a long-term instrument or selling the instrument at a discount.

There are four types of risks you face in the fixed-investment market: interest rate risk, where the price of the bond changes due to interest rate fluctuations; credit risk, where the issuer of your instrument runs into financial adversity; call risk, where the issuer of your debt obligation will exercise the right to repay the debt prior to maturity—an event that could cut short your high rate of return; and inflation risk, where your purchasing power is seriously eroded by inflation. How does each risk lead us to our decision not to recommend tax-exempt securities?

Interest rate risk will be approximately the same for instruments with similar maturities. The credit risk of many municipal agencies, however, will not be the same. Their credit risk has significantly increased, given the budgetary problems at many state and local government agencies. Compare these risks with U.S. government securities, which have no credit risk.

What about call risk? In the municipal bond market, the issuing agencies often have a call provision for early redemption. This substantially reduces your upside potential in a bond. When interest rates go down, your bond will appreciate in value. However, the issuer is more likely to call or redeem your bond. The agency will pay for it with the proceeds of new bonds sold at the lower interest rate. This often reduces the cost significantly, but limits your capital gains. If interest rates go up, you're stuck with a bond that has eroded in value and is no longer giving you a competitive yield. U.S. government bonds and short-term corporate bonds have very limited, if any, call risk.

The inflation risk is significant with all fixed investments. One should not invest in fixed instruments to keep up with inflation. Fixed instruments should be used to build stability into the portfolio. Their percentage of the whole portfolio is a function of your willingness to take risk. Fixed investments protect the downside risk of your account. In addition, fixed investments provide funds to rebalance or reoptimize your portfolio into additional growth investments when a significant down market occurs. We will discuss this strategy in Chapter Twelve.

In addition to their increased risk, tax-exempt securities have much greater trading costs. These additional costs negate using most enhanced strategies such as the matrix pricing strategy—the increased turnover creates a negative added value. When we examine the differences between the taxable and tax-free investments, it is in most investors' best interests to maintain the taxable investments in their asset class portfolio. If market conditions change to favor tax-free investments, repositioning to appropriate funds should be considered. While paying taxes has never been a favorite pastime of any investor, often it can make sense to do so, even with the current tax structure.

EQUITY INVESTMENTS

Deciding which equity investments to include in your asset class portfolio for growth requires some study. You know that the market is efficient—

that there is no ability to do any market timing—so you need to stay fully invested. There is also no ability to select individual securities and expect to beat the market. What should you do?

Earlier in the chapter, we illustrated how the U.S. equity market could be divided into deciles. Let's examine how each of these deciles has performed. In Table 6–8, the equity market is again divided into deciles 1 through 10. On the left-hand column are three-year rolling time periods from 1926 to 1994. The shaded boxes are the decile with either the highest returns of the time period or the lowest returns. In the second row (1929 to 1931), the 1st decile had a −26.79 percent return, but the 10th decile had a −49.69 percent return. So, the 1st decile was the best and the 10th was the worst, even though all deciles were negative for the period.

In the next three-year period, 1932 to 1934, the 1st decile had a 10.61 percent return, but the 10th had a 60.77 percent return, so they flip-flopped from the previous period. Now the 10th decile is doing the best, and the 1st decile is doing the worst. If you just scan the chart, you can see that the shaded boxes are at one end or the other of the table for the most part—which means you're getting the most action, good or bad, either in large company stocks or in very small company stocks. This chart highlights how these groups of stocks behave differently.

We recommend that investors currently place their domestic equity asset class stocks in U.S. companies with the largest capitalizations and in U.S. small company stocks in the 9th and 10th deciles. These asset classes have proved to have the most impact on the entire U.S. market's performance. Academic research shows that the largest and smallest companies' stocks have low correlation with each other. Building a portfolio containing asset classes with low correlation to each other results in greater long-term performance for the investor while reducing risk through diversification.

To implement these recommendations, you should consider investing in index funds that attempt to replicate Standard & Poor's 500 and the Russell 2000 index. Through recent enhancement, institutional investors have been able to add significant value through different strategies with new asset class funds. In Chapter Nine, we will discuss one method for improving on U.S. large company stock funds with dramatic success. For now, however, let's look at a trading strategy that adds value in U.S. small company stocks.

TABLE 6-8
Annualized Stock Returns (%) by Decile, 1926-94

| | | | | | NYSE decile | | | | | |
Time	1	2	3	4	5	6	7	8	9	10
1926-28	28.26	25.90	20.56	26.30	29.43	19.28	21.41	17.31	21.25	20.84
1929-31	-26.79	-33.06	-35.65	-36.69	-37.13	-39.95	-40.56	-44.77	-49.31	-49.69
1932-34	10.61	23.85	28.86	29.73	20.19	31.19	27.63	41.35	41.23	60.77
1935-37	8.18	9.19	2.29	4.19	8.67	5.36	10.56	3.58	12.48	8.75
1938-40	6.09	4.18	7.06	8.38	12.48	12.87	9.73	8.42	2.44	-8.47
1941-43	7.81	15.31	14.88	15.83	16.79	16.48	24.75	30.31	33.47	55.46
1944-46	13.41	20.83	20.04	24.02	26.46	27.15	25.86	28.90	35.59	38.61
1947-49	9.08	8.24	8.13	6.80	6.35	5.48	3.55	3.85	2.70	4.61
1950-52	21.39	22.71	19.15	20.93	19.15	20.16	21.50	21.81	18.59	18.39
1953-55	24.38	22.12	22.88	20.60	22.74	24.38	21.46	20.77	22.81	24.74
1956-58	10.63	15.09	13.03	15.57	14.92	10.70	15.41	14.45	15.26	13.18
1959-61	12.49	13.19	15.98	14.40	14.44	13.45	14.41	13.82	14.32	14.76
1962-64	8.25	6.73	6.65	5.63	2.63	3.73	5.12	5.33	3.63	4.46
1965-67	5.96	10.85	16.40	19.58	22.86	25.18	26.15	30.21	33.33	39.51
1968-70	1.26	1.83	3.27	2.30	0.04	0.41	1.36	3.70	-6.39	-3.05
1971-73	7.22	0.82	0.33	.034	-3.60	-3.54	-5.58	-7.42	-10.65	-10.01
1974-76	4.19	11.62	13.04	15.90	14.55	14.77	17.17	20.00	19.55	22.46
1977-79	4.59	8.63	13.38	16.87	19.79	22.82	25.26	25.05	27.75	34.74
1980-82	13.47	17.36	19.00	20.07	20.92	22.18	20.17	20.56	20.16	19.41
1983-85	19.06	20.53	18.34	16.96	17.23	19.04	19.52	18.32	16.87	11.94
1986-88	12.32	13.30	13.20	13.04	11.13	8.23	8.39	6.80	3.07	0.74
1989-91	19.44	16.48	18.01	16.52	14.85	13.40	14.44	9.39	8.43	2.26
1992-94	4.62	8.26	9.34	9.07	13.50	12.46	13.02	9.43	11.17	18.31

The costs of trading in the 9th and 10th deciles are significant. A mutual fund manager who wants to place any significant amount of capital in this area will find that the trading cost is not just the bid/ask spread but also the market impact of his orders. Even index funds run into this problem and often underperform their indexes by a wide margin due to this increased cost.

If you managed a pure index fund, you would have to buy stocks at the ask price and sell them at the bid price. Your parameters state that you have to match the index exactly. Whatever the index does, you want to do. You are trying to follow the index as closely as possible in terms of pricing. Now, what happens under the decile strategy? If you want to buy a block of 300,000 shares of a 9th decile stock and it is trading at $10, that comes to $3 million. Remember that the average daily trading volume for a 9th decile stock is approximately $280,000. Are you going to be able to buy it at the ask price? Of course not; at this volume you will move the market. For an active mutual fund manager, this is much worse; he is usually placing much larger bets in concentrated issues and trading much more often. This can easily work out to an underperformance of the market of 5 percent or more.

A few institutional asset class funds have successfully implemented a strategy that significantly reduces trading costs, to capture the small company stock effect. This is accomplished by utilization of a discount block trading strategy and a willingness to be slightly overweight or underweight on any particular stock in the index. In Figure 6–9, we can see a typical block trade, which illustrates that the sellers of block trades are willing to absorb a discount bid.

In this example, a major shareholder wanted to sell 351,000 shares, or 3.2 percent of the company. The company's market capitalization on this date was $106 million. The average daily trading volume for the previous month had been 15,600 shares. Prior to the trade, the last sale had been 9⅝, with the current bid 9⅝ and the current ask 9¾. The shareholder sold his shares to the institutional asset class mutual fund manager not at the ask price of 9¾, not at the bid price of 9⅝, but for 9⅜, a trade value of $3.3 million. The trading cost was -3.9%. The trading cost is calculated by the bid/ask spread. The bid price was 9⅝ and the ask price to the institutional asset class fund provider was 9⅜. The trading cost was therefore (9⅜–9¾) or –⅜ percent. This represents a savings of 3.9 percent (⅜ divided by the ask price of 9¾). Why would the shareholder sell at this discount? Liquidity. If he had placed the order on the market, he would have driven the market price down significantly due to the relatively large trade size.

FIGURE 6–9
An Example of a Small Company Stock Trade

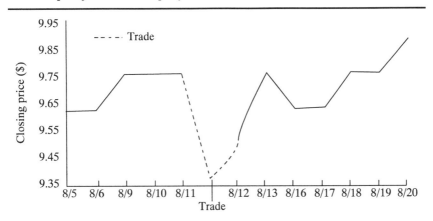

Utilizing a discount block trading strategy allows an institutional asset class mutual fund to realize the small company stock effect without the significant trading costs. The negative 3.9 percent cost to the shareholder represents a positive 3.9 percent return to the investors in the fund. It is through these enhancements that institutional asset class mutual fund managers can achieve a comparative advantage for their clients without trying to predict the market. These advantages are now available to you.

ENDNOTES

[1]This was calculated by screening the Morningstar OnDisc Database as of December 31, 1994, for the average total operating expenses of all equity mutual funds. On that date there were 2,773 equity mutual funds.

[2]Elton, Edwin J.; Martin J. Gruber; Sanjiv Das; and Matthew Hlavka, "Efficiency with Costly Information: A Reinterpretation of Evidence from Managed Portfolios," *The Society for Financial Studies,* 1993.

[3]The difference between the expected and actual rates of return on a mutual fund is called *alpha,* denoted as α. Using the Capital Asset Pricing Model, we can calculate the excess returns that the mutual fund earned above the market. If the market's return was 10 percent, the mutual fund's return was 14 percent, the mutual fund's beta (β) was 1.2, and the Treasury-bill rate was 6 percent, then the mutual fund's alpha was $\alpha = 14 - [\beta(10-6)+6] = 3.2$ percent. As we discussed in Chapter Three, CAPM does not accurately measure excess performance due to its single risk factor—the market. When the Fama–French three-factor model is used, most mutual funds have negative alphas.

[4]This was calculated by screening the Morningstar OnDisc Database as of December 31, 1994, for the average turnover of all equity mutual funds. On that date there were 2,773 equity mutual funds.

[5]Elton, Edwin J.; Martin J. Gruber; Sanjiv Das; and Matthew Hlavka, "Efficiency with Costly Information: A Reinterpretation of Evidence from Managed Portfolios," *The Society for Financial Studies,* 1993.

[6]Shoven, John B. and Joel M. Dickson, "Ranking Mutual Funds on an After–Tax Basis," Stanford University Center for Economic Policy Research Discussion Paper, no. 344.

[7]Jeffrey, Robert H., and Robert D. Arnott, "Is Your Alpha Big Enough to Cover Its Taxes?" *Journal of Portfolio Management* (Spring 1993).

[8]This was calculated by screening the Morningstar OnDisc Database as of December 31, 1994, for mutual funds that were either index funds or enhanced index funds and were not institutional funds nor restricted access funds. On that date, and using these screens, there were 69 asset class mutual funds.

[9]Fama, Eugene F., "Time Varying Expected Returns," unpublished paper (February 1988, updated January 1995).

[10]Ibid.

Chapter Seven

Adding Value through Global Diversification

I n this chapter you will learn how to lower risk and increase returns using international asset classes in your portfolio. Global diversification is the fourth key concept of Asset Class Investing. Generally, professionals take for granted that diversification includes adding international securities to investor portfolios. However, it's not being done to the extent we believe it should be.

Unfortunately, most investors view foreign equity investments suspiciously. Why should they risk diversifying internationally? Even though the academic support for such diversification is compelling, many investors have viewed investing overseas as a gamble. Let's take a dispassionate look at how international markets really work and which international investments should play a part in your asset class portfolio.

World markets can provide broader diversification and access to more asset classes with dissimilar price movements. Today, many world markets rival U.S. markets, both in sophistication and safety. Your understanding of these markets can substantially reduce the risk in your portfolio while enhancing your returns.

Which international asset classes should you include in your global diversification? We will review three major candidates for inclusion: international fixed-income, international equity, and emerging market asset classes.

INTERNATIONAL FIXED-INCOME ASSETS

The fixed-income component of your investment portfolio is included primarily to mitigate the risk in your equity allocation. So, as we discussed with domestic fixed-income asset classes, you should be only interested in the highest-quality securities. The major foreign government bond markets have limited default risk. For that reason, you would look only at those countries that have very active markets and little political risk. As Figure 7–1 shows, in 1989 the world's government bond market capitalization was over $6 trillion.[1]

FIGURE 7–1
World's Government Bond Market Capitalization

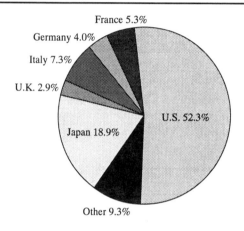

Total capitalization: $6 trillion.

You have two more decisions to make. First, should you have any international fixed-income asset classes in your portfolio? Second, should they be hedged? *Hedging* is the technique of investing in an asset with a return pattern that offsets your exposure to a different source of risk. The risk you would be hedging in using the foreign exchange markets is currency risk. This is an important point. If you purchase bonds internationally in that country's currency, you not only take the risk associated with domestic bonds, you add an additional risk from fluctuating currency exchange rates.

If you believe that markets are efficient, then currency risk should be reflected in the bond price, and that component would be equal to the cost of hedging. Investors who accept currency risk enter into speculation, not investing. This speculation is based on their ability to predict the relative movement between that country's currency and that of the United States. The currency market is very efficient. To believe that anyone has superior knowledge and can judge which way currencies will move is speculative and introduces more risk to your portfolio. Currency speculation is a "zero-sum game."

In a zero-sum game, if one player wins, another has to lose. The only way a new player can make a bet is if someone bets against the new player. It's much like a casino, where the house takes a piece of each bet as a commission. On average, the only one that comes out a winner is the house. Prudent investors don't participate in zero-sum games; speculators do.

Let's look at a practical example. You own a Japanese bond, and the U.S. dollar gains 10 percent against the Japanese currency, while interest rates remain the same. You have suffered a 10 percent capital loss on this bond. Had you purchased a futures contract, you could have eliminated the currency risk, but at the price of a foreign-exchange contract. Since you now know that markets are efficient, it make sense to hedge foreign fixed-income securities. The risk of not hedging would not be rewarded by the market and would substantially increase the volatility of the portfolio compared with a hedged portfolio.

How does the interaction of hedged and unhedged portfolios affect investors? Let's take a look at some time series data on fixed-income markets in Canada, France, Germany, Japan, the United Kingdom, and the United States. Reviewing the period from 1987 through 1993, we select two portfolios equally balanced globally, with one portfolio hedged, the other unhedged (see Table 7–1). We find that the hedged global portfolio had less risk than the unhedged portfolio of similar duration. *Duration* is the effective maturity of a bond. It is defined as the weighted average of the times until each payment is made, with the weights proportional to the present value of the payments. The unhedged portfolio should be unacceptable to you because of its increased risk.

TABLE 7–1
Risk Measures of Fixed-Income Strategies, 1987–1993

	Global Hedged	Global Unhedged[*]	Five-Year Treasury Index	Lehman Index
Standard deviation (%)	4.05	9.01	4.57	4.68
Duration	5.5	5.5	4.37	5.34

Standard deviation annualized from monthly data.
[*]Equal weighted portfolio of Lehman Country Indexes: United States, United Kingdom, Japan, France, Germany, and Canada.

Dissimilar price movements between asset classes is the primary method for risk reduction. If you hedge your international bond portfolio, you still have bonds that tend not to move together. If you examine each of the hedged countries' indexes in Table 7–2, you will see that they have relatively low correlations; they do not move in tandem.

TABLE 7–2
Correlations of Hedged Countries' Bond Indexes, 1987–1993

	Canada	France	Germany	Japan	United Kingdom	United States
Canada	1.00					
France	0.36	1.00				
Germany	0.46	0.77	1.00			
Japan	0.45	0.36	0.45	1.00		
United Kingdom	0.54	0.51	0.53	0.50	1.00	
United States	0.64	0.37	0.44	0.41	0.37	1.00

If you considered the correlations in Table 7–2 in isolation, you would want to include hedged foreign bonds in your portfolio. The hedged global bond portfolio has a standard deviation approaching that of U.S. five-year government bonds for the same time period (4.57 percent) or of Lehman's corporate government index (4.68 percent). The hedged global bond portfolio has a longer duration. This approximately equal standard deviation and low correlation warrants at least consideration of adding the international fixed-income asset class fund to your portfolio.

At this time, however, the cost of operating global hedged bond funds and their trading costs—including the custodial, duty, and hedging costs—make the benefit of inclusion minimal at best and often complicate matters. *We recommend at this time that your asset class portfolio not include the international fixed-income asset class.* This decision should be reevaluated each year with your advisor as additional institutional asset class funds become available.

INTERNATIONAL EQUITY ASSETS

In 1960, the world equity markets were valued at slightly below $500 billion; the U.S. portion of these markets was 73 percent (see Figure 7–2).

FIGURE 7–2
World Equity Markets, 1960

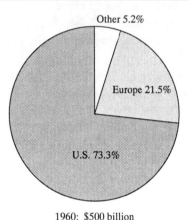

1960: $500 billion

By 1990, the value of the world equity markets had risen sixteenfold, to approximately $8.3 trillion.[2] The U.S. market grew, but not as fast as the rest of the world's markets. The U.S. share of world equity markets had shrunk to 33 percent (see Figure 7–3).

FIGURE 7–3
World Equity Markets, 1990

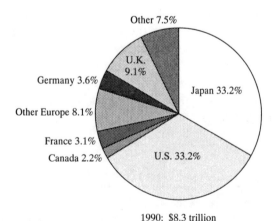

1990: $8.3 trillion

When you consider the inclusion of international equity asset classes in your portfolio, you are looking to see if their addition would reduce risk. The international equity markets and the U.S. equity markets have a low correlation; they do not move in tandem. Figure 7–4 shows how international diversification affects the relationship between risk and return. It illustrates the trade-off of returns and risk as we include more of the international equity market.

FIGURE 7–4

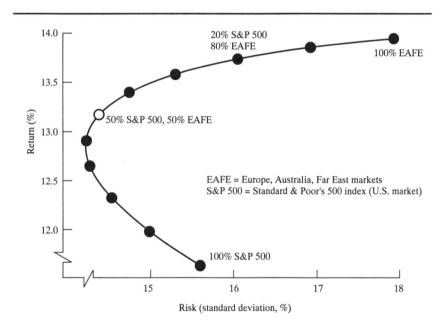

The higher the point is on the chart, the higher the return; the further to the left a point is, the lower its risk. In Figure 7–4, we illustrate that for the 20-year period ending December 31, 1994, investors achieved a higher rate of return with less volatility by owning international stocks in addition to U.S. equities. We produced this graph by first starting with the S&P 500 index and assuming a 100 percent investment. Then we reduced the allocation by 10 percent at each subsequent point and placed that 10 percent in Morgan Stanley's Europe, Australia, Far East index (EAFE) until we reached 100 percent exposure to EAFE. EAFE is the most commonly used index for representing the international market, much like the S&P 500 is used to represent the U.S. equity market. The optimum return during this time period—that which gives us the highest return relative to the risk assumed—occurred when 50 percent of the portfolio was invested in the U.S. equity market and 50 percent overseas.

The breakdown of EAFE worldwide is shown in Table 7–3.

TABLE 7–3
EAFE's Worldwide Coverage

Category	Countries	Number of Issues in EAFE
Japan	Japan	266
Pacific Rim (except Japan)	Hong Kong	39
	Singapore	32
	Malaysia	68
	Australia	52
	Korea	0
United Kingdom	United Kingdom	146
Continental Europe	France	68
	Germany	67
	Italy	72
	Switzerland	57
	Netherlands	21
	Belgium	20
	Spain	36
Total Asia and Europe		**944**

As of December 31, 1994.

You should include an EAFE asset class fund in your portfolio. EAFE, like most performance measurement indexes, is a weighted market capitalization. This will tend to overstate the weight of Japan. There, it is common for publicly traded companies to invest in the stocks of other companies, and these "cross-holdings" will be counted twice.[3] In the institutional asset class fund we utilize for our investors, exposure to Japan's stocks is held to 38 percent to compensate for this overweighting. You should do this in your own portfolio.

ARE INTERNATIONAL MARKETS EFFICIENT?

Many managers argue that the international markets are less efficient. Fortunately for you, that does not appear to be the case. You do not have to waste time identifying the superstars among the international equity mutual funds. Prices overseas quickly adjust to new information, consistent with the Modern Portfolio Theory. There appear to be no credible studies that show consistently superior performance by active managers in any major international market.[4]

WHAT ABOUT THE COSTS OF INVESTING OVERSEAS?

The active managers of international equities will still argue that the markets are not perfectly efficient. Even if they were correct, which they are not, the trading costs of capturing these pricing inefficiencies would negate most of the benefits. In Table 7–4, the costs have been estimated on a trade of $50,000 for each of the countries. Trading costs include commissions, stamp duties, and custodial charges. They range from a high of 139 basis points in Singapore/Malaysia to a low of 38 basis points in the Netherlands.

TABLE 7–4
Estimated International Agency Costs (in Basis Points)

Country	Commissions	Stamp Duty	Custodial Transaction	Total Basis Points
Japan	65	0	7	72
Australia	75	30	17	122
Hong Kong	60	36	24	120
Singapore/Malaysia	100	15	24	139
United Kingdom	50	50	9	109
France	50	30	7	87
Germany	50	13	8	71
Italy	50	0	40	90
Switzerland	40	9	13	62
Netherlands	35	0	3	38
Belgium	90	20	15	125
Spain	70	0	5	75

Source: *Dimensional Fund Advisors.*
Based on buy-side trades and an average estimated trade size of $50,000.
As of June 30, 1993.

Given the already high fixed costs of international investing, high turnover rates for international portfolios can have a severe effect on returns.

The significantly higher costs of investing overseas for U.S. investors makes it even more important for you to be aware of the turnover ratio of the international mutual fund you use. An active manager trying to be competitive in Singapore with a 200 percent turnover would experience a 2.78 percent cost of doing business, without consideration of any market impact. Combining these costs with the average expense ratio of international equity mutual funds of 1.80 percent[5] results in a total cost to the investor of 4.58 percent. The benefit of active trading does not justify its costs.

WHAT ABOUT THE SIZE EFFECT?

Conventional wisdom recommends that investors have a balanced approach to investing. Typically, this recommendation is 60 percent in the S&P 500 index and 40 percent in Treasury bonds. In Table 7–5, we call this portfolio P1. If we use P1 as our benchmark, we can introduce new asset classes to the portfolio and see how they perform. The goal is to build portfolios that have higher returns at the same level of risk.

TABLE 7–5
Increasing International Exposure

	P1 %	P2 %	P3 %	P4 %	P5 %
Portfolio Makeup					
S&P 500 index	60	55	50	45	46
EAFE index	0	5	10	15	15
Treasury bills	40	40	40	40	39
Performance Measures					
Annualized return	9.5	9.5	9.6	9.7	9.7
Standard deviation	9.8	9.7	9.7	9.7	9.9

With each portfolio, we reallocate 5 percent from the S&P 500 to EAFE index. In P2 the return does not increase but the risk is reduced, allowing us to reallocate more. In P3, the 10 percent allocation has a slight increase in return, with no change in risk. By the time we allocate 15 percent to the EAFE, we have the optimum return enhancement to the portfolio given the risk level of our 60/40 benchmark. This minimal benefit in itself does not seem to justify allocating anything to EAFE.

If we introduce an international small company stock asset class and a government/corporate bond asset class, we can achieve significant improvement, as Table 7–6 illustrates.

TABLE 7–6
Increasing International Exposure (continued)

| | Portfolio | | | | |
| | P6 | P7 | P8 | P9 | P10 |
	%	%	%	%	–%
Portfolio Makeup					
S&P 500 index	60	45	45	45	45
EAFE index	0	15	10	5	0
Intl' small company	0	0	5	10	15
Govt./corp. index	40	40	40	40	40
Performance Measures					
Annualized return	13.5	14.0	14.4	14.8	15.2
Standard deviation	9.8	9.5	9.3	9.1	9.0

This effect is due to small company stocks having a relatively low correlation with large company stocks, not only in the United States but internationally as well. Adding small company stocks increases the effectiveness of our diversification.. The size effect works for both domestic and international stocks. Your *equity* portfolio should include an international small company asset class.

CURRENCY RISK IN EQUITY ASSET CLASS FUNDS

Many international mutual funds utilize hedging in their equity asset classes. These foreign hedging strategies can be divided into two basic types. The first is a bet that there is a premium paid to investors for taking the foreign exchange risk. The second is a bet on the relative direction of the next movement in the foreign currency exchange rate. Several studies point out that the market does not pay a premium associated with the foreign exchange risk,[6] and it does not make sense for you to speculate on the direction of foreign exchange price movements, as we discussed under fixed-income assets. *We recommend that your international equity asset classes be unhedged for foreign exchange risk.*

EMERGING MARKETS

Many advisors are considering the addition of the small, emerging markets in their clients' portfolios. With the United States and Japan together representing more than half the world equity market capitalization, the potential of finding other countries that are emerging can be exciting—the next new investment market success—if only you can get in on the ground floor. There seems to be no shortage of possibilities; There are now more than 40 stock markets in the European communities alone. In South America, Asia, and even Africa, new, emerging stock markets are growing rapidly. Very high expected rates of return and even higher volatility characterize these exciting markets. However, the lack of liquidity, difficult entry for foreigners, high cost structures, and political risks make this asset class unsuitable for most investors' asset class portfolio.

In Chapter Six, we recommended that your portfolio include a money market, a one-year corporate, a five-year U.S. government, a U.S. large company, and a U.S. small company asset class mutual fund. In this chapter, we have added to your recommended portfolio an international large company and an international small company asset class mutual fund. The next chapter will show you how to put them all together to build your own portfolio, or you can use one of the model portfolios we have provided.

ENDNOTES

[1]*How Big Is the World Bond Market? 1990 Update* (New York: Salomon Brothers, 1990).

[2]Ibbotson, Roger G. and Gary P. Brinson, *Global Investing—The Professional's Guide to the World Capital Markets* (New York: McGraw Hill, 1993).

[3]McDonald, J. "The Mochiai Effect: Japanese Corporate Cross-Holdings" *Journal of Portfolio Management* (Fall 1989), pp. 90–94.

[4]Hawawini, G.A., *European Equity Markets: Price Behavior and Efficiency,* Monograph of the Salomon Brothers Center for the Study of Financial Institutions (New York University, 1984).

[5]This was calculated by screening the Morningstar OnDisc Database as of December 31, 1994, for all international equity funds that were deemed foreign and not institutional or restricted-access funds. On that date there were 190 equity mutual funds that met these criteria.

[6]Perold, A., and E. Shulman, "The Free Lunch in Currency Hedging: Implications for Investment Policy and Performance Standards," *Financial Analysts Journal* (May–June 1990), pp. 45-50.

Chapter Eight

How to Build the Optimal Portfolio

You now have seven basic building blocks: a money market, a one-year corporate, a five-year U.S. government, a U.S. large company stock, a U.S. small company stock, an international large company stock, and an international small company stock asset class mutual fund. How do you determine the optimal combination of these asset classes for your portfolio?

THE FIVE STEPS IN ALLOCATING YOUR PORTFOLIO AMONG ASSET CLASSES

1. Determine the expected rate of return. Before you invest in any asset, you should know what you expect to make. You want to know that the expected rate of return justifies the inclusion of that investment. The expected rate is the target rate of return against which you can measure your realized performance.

2. Know what risk the asset class has. Risk is the uncertainty of future rates of return. The historical volatility or risk of an investment can be statistically measured using its standard deviation. The current price of the security reflects the expected total return of an investment and its perceived risk. The lower the risk, the lower the return.

3. Calculate the correlation coefficients of all the asset classes. Correlation coefficients measure the dissimilar price movements among asset classes. Correlation coefficients quantify the probability of two or more investments moving in the same direction at the same time. Values range from +1 to −1. A correlation coefficient of +1 implies that the returns of the assets move in lockstep with each other, although not necessarily by equal increments. A measure of −1 means they move in opposite directions, at the same time.

The use of low or negative correlation is a powerful tool in providing effective diversification. Many institutional asset class mutual funds, representing total market segments, have historically shown a pattern of moving dissimilarly in time, degree, or direction. When these institutional asset class mutual funds are combined, they reduce the volatility of the portfolio.

4. Solve for the optimal combination of asset classes for each level of risk. Once expected returns, standard deviations, and correlation coefficients have been determined, optimized portfolios can be created. Connecting all the optimal portfolios forms the "efficient frontier" line. The efficient frontier line represents the asset class mix with the highest expected rate of return for each given level of risk. More about that later. Prudent investors restrict their choice of portfolios to those appearing on the efficient frontier and representing their own risk-tolerance level.

5. Identify your risk tolerance. Many advisors have developed questionnaires to quantify the risk level investors are willing to take. Typically, they utilize various qualitative measures. We have found that these measures are subjective at best and are influenced significantly by how you feel the day you complete the questionnaire. We like the quantitative approach; it's much more effective and reliable.

The technique we use is to determine what your portfolio would have done during 1973 and 1974. For example, assume that your portfolio lost 30 percent during the 1973–74 period and you had $200,000 invested. That means your portfolio decreased to $140,000. Would you have closed your account because of the downturn and fired your financial advisor? Probably, if you didn't understand the risks ahead of time. You are in control if you predetermine the risk level that you are willing to accept. Over the long term, the more risk you take, the higher the rate of return, but only if you stay with the strategy. In Chapter Ten we will return to this strategy when we discuss building your investment policy statement.

DOING THE CALCULATIONS

Many investors can get sidetracked by formulas. This math can sometimes seem overwhelming and complicated. We have included the formulas for calculating expected returns, standard deviations and correlation coefficients in the Appendix. Since most investors are working with advisors, most of you do not need to know how to calculate each of the five steps. You just need to understand the end result.

Expected Rates of Return

In calculating the expected rates of return for each asset class, investors must recognize that these are theoretical returns. In developing your portfolio, the expected rate of return of each asset class is the annual mean (average) forecasted for the next five years. If you are going to invest in a portfolio that includes equities, the time horizon should be at least five years. The expected rate of return should be recalculated at least once annually. As mentioned above, in the Appendix we have included the mathematical formulas that we utilize to accomplish this. Table 8–1 shows expected returns for each asset class.

TABLE 8–1
Expected Returns for Preferred Asset Classes

Asset Class	Expected Returns %
Money market	6.1
One-year corporate	7.9
Five-year government	9.3
U.S. large company	14.5
U.S. small company	20.6
International large company	16.9
International small company	18.3

Expected Risk

In Table 8–2, we illustrate the historical standard deviations and the time periods we used.

TABLE 8–2
Historical Standard Deviations for Preferred Asset Classes

Asset Class	Years	Annualized Standard Deviation %
Money market	1926–1994	3.3
One-year corporate	1971–1994	4.0
Five-year U.S. government	1926–1994	5.7
U.S. large company stocks	1926–1994	20.3
U.S. small company stocks	1926–1994	39.0
Intl. large company stocks	1970–1994	27.5
Intl. small company stocks	1970–1994	31.5

Correlation Coefficients

The most important component of investing is understanding correlation coefficients. Common sense dictates that we don't "put all our eggs in one basket." By combining assets with low correlations, we can lower the overall portfolio risk while enhancing the risk-adjusted rates of return. In analyzing the correlation coefficients of the asset classes, we must use the period represented by the asset class that has the shortest time series of information. Table 8–3 illustrates the correlation coefficients for each of the asset classes we are considering for our portfolio for the time period from 1972 through 1994.

TABLE 8–3
Correlation Coefficients for Preferred Asset Classes

	Money Market	One-Year Corp.	Five-Year Govt.	United States Large Co.	United States Small Co.	International Large Co.	International Small Co.
Money market	1.000						
One-year corporate	.915	1.000					
Five-year U.S. government	.531	.771	1.000				
U.S. large company stocks	.003	.062	.263	1.000			
U.S. small company stocks	.055	.000	.139	.766	1.000		
Intl. large company stocks	.253	.231	.083	.594	.474	1.000	
Intl. small company stocks	.286	.331	.233	.391	.316	.909	1.000

Now that we've calculated the expected rates of return, the standard deviations and the correlations of each of our asset classes, we have to determine the optimal combination of investments that gives us the highest rate of return for each level of risk.

After expected returns, standard deviations (risk), and correlation coefficients (dissimilar price movements) have been determined for each asset class, optimal portfolios can be calculated for every level of risk. These portfolios lie on a graph line called the *efficient frontier*, which represents the asset class mixes with the highest expected returns for each level of risk. By plotting every portfolio representing a given level of risk and highest expected return, we are able to trace a line connecting all of the efficient portfolios. This line forms the efficient frontier. Portfolios such as the Standard & Poor's 500 index that fall below the line can have rates of return comparable to a portfolio on the line. However, they would be less desirable because they would have higher risk, as measured by their standard deviations. Because the line represents the highest return for any level of risk, there can be no portfolios above the line.

FIGURE 8–1
Efficient Frontier

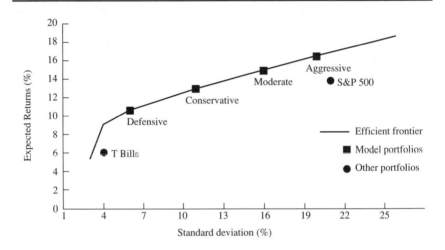

THE EFFICIENT FRONTIER

In Figure 8–1, we have illustrated how the efficient frontier would be plotted for our asset mixes. We have identified four model portfolios along the efficient frontier. For lack of better terms, we have called them Defensive, Conservative, Moderate, and Aggressive. Their equity allocations are 25, 50, 70, and 85 percent, respectively. While the terms Defensive, Conservative, Moderate, and Aggressive mean different things to each of us, they are convenient working titles for various combinations of asset classes.

Once you determine your risk tolerance, you can then look on the efficient frontier line and select the model portfolio that suits you. Don't be swayed by what we call the "model portfolio." Each investor has his or her own risk tolerance. It is the trade-off between the risk the investor is willing to take to receive a specific expected rate of return.

Generally, younger people have the greatest tolerance for risk and retirees the least. Often, younger people feel that they have both time and earning capability to recover from any loss, while retirees may feel they do not. Retired individuals are dependent on income from their investment principal, and any loss would represent a reduction in income. However, as investors become more sophisticated and understand Asset Class Investing, they are often more comfortable with risk because they understand that investing for the long term will mitigate the volatility of their portfolios as a whole.

In evaluating the correct risk tolerance, any financial analyst can provide you with a long, qualitative questionnaire asking you how you feel about the market. The reality is that questionnaires are subjective, and your responses will depend on how you're feeling about the market that day—whether it's up or down, or whether you are up or down. Using historical information, we are able to illustrate how these funds performed in the past. From that, we can simulate the past performance of our model portfolios and make some assumptions about future performance. In Table 8–3 we have shown the proportion of each of these asset classes in the four model portfolios.

TABLE 8–4
Composition of Model Portfolios

Asset Class	Defensive	Conservative	Moderate	Aggressive
Money market	5%	5%	5%	5%
One-year corporate	30%	20%	20%	10%
Five-year U.S. government	40%	25%	5%	0%
U.S. large company stocks	15%	20%	25%	25%
U.S. small company stocks	0%	5%	10%	15%
International large company stocks	10%	20%	25%	25%
International small company stocks	0%	5%	10%	20%

In Figures 8–2 through 8–5, we have illustrated the performance over 1-year, 5-year, and 10-year periods. To determine your own risk tolerance, look at the annual performance of the model portfolios from 1973 and 1974. Would you have stayed with those investments? If not, reduce your risk by considering the model portfolio with the next lower equity exposure. If the answer is yes, consider moving up in risk to the portfolio with the next higher equity exposure.

FIGURE 8–2
Defensive Portfolio 1972–1994

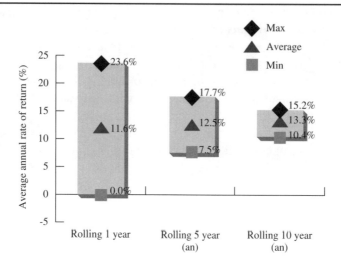

FIGURE 8–3
Conservative Portfolio 1972–1994

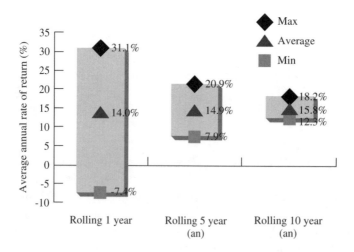

FIGURE 8–4
Moderate Portfolio 1972–1994

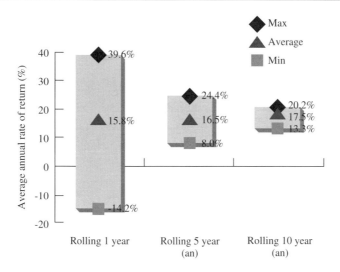

FIGURE 8–5
Aggressive Portfolio 1972–1994

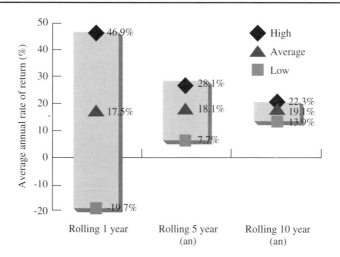

Notice the five-year performance numbers. From 1972–94, there was never a five-year period when the model asset class portfolios did not have positive returns. In each five-year period, the returns always outperformed Treasury bonds. This is the way Asset Class Investing works. If investors have a time horizon of more than five years, they can ride through business cycles with peace of mind knowing that the free markets are working for them.

You should notice that Figures 8–2 through 8–5 are different from most Wall Street presentations. They include the 1970s. Even *Morningstar*, one of the premier mutual fund reporting publications, only goes back to 1976. For the financial markets, 1973 and 1974 were the worst recession years since World War II. In selecting the risk tolerance that's appropriate for you, consider your potential optimal portfolio at its average risk level, including its performance during 1973 and 1974. Just because Wall Street doesn't acknowledge the existence of those years doesn't mean you shouldn't consider them.

Let's review where we are. We've examined the five key concepts of Asset Class Investing: (1) effective diversification; (2) dissimilar price movements; (3) institutional asset class mutual funds; (4) global diversification; and (5) building the optimal portfolio. In the next chapter we'll examine additional strategies that the academic community believes will further enhance your investment success.

Chapter Nine

The Three-Factor Model

O ur knowledge of how financial markets work is constantly improving, and to maximize your performance you have to stay on the frontier of that knowledge. Many investment mutual fund providers have used this idea to introduce enhanced index funds. These enhanced index funds can improve your portfolio returns by as much as 3 percent. The Vanguard Group recently introduced a new series of mutual funds to take advantage of this improvement.

In this chapter we will share with you new research to further your understanding of how markets work as you build your portfolio. So far, we have discussed two risks that investors are rewarded for taking: market risk and size risk. We have successfully put this new research to work by investing in large and small company stocks around the world.

In the model portfolios, we have invested in asset classes that have both of these risk factors. But there is a third risk factor that investors are compensated for taking, one we have not yet implemented in the model portfolios. In this chapter, we will show you how to use this risk factor to add more than 300 basis points to your portfolio's performance, with no measurable increase in risk.

It was Eugene Fama—then working with fellow University of Chicago Professor Kenneth French—who uncovered this third risk factor. Fama and French determined that portfolio performance was really attributable to three factors, rather than a single factor.[1] They discovered that it was not simply a matter of how much an investor had in the market alone, but also the amount she or he invested in large and small companies and the third risk factor—(amount placed in stocks with high book-to-market ratios)—that determined investment returns. By gaining an understanding of these three concepts rather than focusing on a single factor, an investor can better design her or his portfolio. These three factors of returns are (1) market risk; (2) company size; and (3) the book-to-market ratio

(BTM). These factors collectively explain 95 percent of the variability of returns an investor can expect.

FACTOR 1: MARKET RISK

Market risk is the risk experienced when investing in the equity market as a whole. Investors demand more than the risk-free rate of return to compensate for the increased risk of holding equities. Greater returns are demanded to compensate for the extra risk.

FACTOR 2: SIZE RISK

Small company stocks have significantly greater risk than large company stocks. Small companies are small because they have limited resources. They are less able to weather downturns in the market. Investors demand a higher rate of return for the risk of investing in smaller companies. The market prices each security in accordance with its risk factor.

FACTOR 3: BOOK-TO-MARKET RISK

Fama and French concluded that the third risk factor could best be identified by companies with a high book value relative to their current market value. These companies are viewed as being out of favor; perhaps because they may be in distress. The book-to-market ratio (BTM) relates the value of a given company using generally accepted accounting principles, with the market value assigned by the stock market. BTM is a ratio comparing the book value of a share of common stock with its market price.

Fama and French found that investors react very differently to companies that have either high BTM or low BTM. Just by knowing which one to include in your portfolio, you can beat the market. High BTM companies are unpopular with investors; investors demand a higher expected rate of return to compensate them for the perceived higher risk. At the end of 1994, IBM was a high-BTM stock, whereas Microsoft had a high market price relative to its book value. Microsoft is the more popular of the two. IBM is viewed by the market as a riskier investment. Why? Investors understand that low-BTM companies (like Microsoft) on average will continue to do well, while companies in distress—high BTM companies like

IBM—on average will continue to do poorly. Investors want to be compensated for this risk. They are not looking for a turnaround situation, because on average that does not happen. They want to be compensated for the likelihood that high-BTM companies will not improve significantly.

In order for you to take advantage of this groundbreaking research, you need to accept the idea that you will earn higher rates of return owning stocks from companies that do poorly! This is counterintuitive to most investors. We have always known that we want to own nothing but the best companies. Thousands of analysts do nothing but try to identify these great companies for you. If only you could build a portfolio of nothing but excellent companies, wouldn't you be assured of investment success?

FIGURE 9–1
Excellent vs. Unexcellent Company Ratios

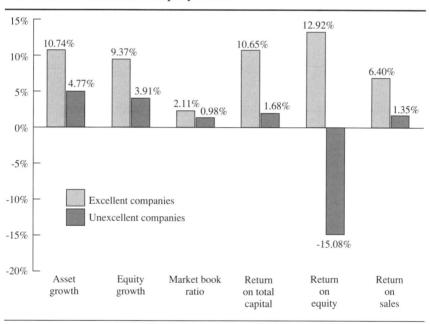

Source: Michele Clayton, "In Search of Excellence: The Investor's Viewpoint," Financial Analysts Journal (May–June 1987), p. 63.

Michele Clayton raised this same question.[2] Her article is based on the best-selling book *In Search of Excellence,* by Thomas Peters and Robert Waterman. Clayton sets out to track the performances of the excellent companies described in the book as well as companies in their peer group that are truly "unexcellent" in their financial performance ratios. First, she examined several traditional business ratios used by fundamental analysts. Without exception, on average, the excellent companies have much higher ratios than the unexcellent companies. In Figure 9–1, we show her findings.

FIGURE 9–2
Actual Performance of Excellent vs. Unexcellent Portfolios

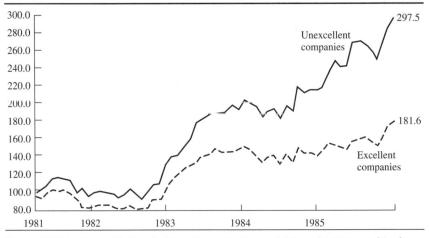

Source: Michele Clayton, "In Search of Excellence: The Investor's Viewpoint," *Financial Analysts Journal* (May–June 1987), p. 63.

Figure 9–2 shows the cumulative return that investors would have received if they had invested $100 in two portfolios, one made up of all the excellent companies and the other of all the unexcellent companies. Contrary to your intuition and most investment advice, the unexcellent companies significantly outperformed the excellent companies. This performance can be explained by the former's high-BTM risk factor.

BUILDING A HIGH-BTM ASSET CLASS

To achieve an optimally diversified asset class portfolio, you must take each of these three risk factors into consideration. The first two risk factors characterize several asset class mutual funds available, as we have discussed in Chapters Six and Seven. Let's examine how a high-BTM asset class can be constructed.

Previously, we divided all NYSE stocks into deciles based on their respective market capitalization (see Chapter Six). This time, we will divide the NYSE stocks by their book-to-market ratios. In Table 9–1, the 1,760 companies on the NYSE are divided into 10 equal groups based on their respective book-to-market ratios. The American Stock Exchange (AMEX) and NASDAQ issues are added to the NYSE decile groupings. Excluded from the table are those companies that did not have available book-value data, such as American Depository Receipts, closed-end issues, or negative book-value firms. This resulted in fewer companies than in 1992, when the study was completed by Fama and French based on market capitalization.

Stocks in the 1st through 3rd deciles were considered low-BTM stocks or growth stocks. Stocks in the 8th through 10th deciles were considered high-BTM stocks or value stocks. Federal Signal Corporation would have had the lowest BTM of all companies on the NYSE, 0.203 as of December 31, 1993. This means that its book value was only 20.3 percent of its current market capitalization. It was clearly a growth stock. Martech USA Inc. would represent the opposite end of the spectrum. Its book value was 1,310.0 percent of its market capitalization. It was a value stock. Standard & Poor's 500 index would have an approximate book-to-market ratio of 0.49.

TABLE 9–1
Value as Defined by Book-to-Market Decile

Book-to-Market Deciles	BTM	NYSE Name	NYSE	AMEX	Natl. NASDAQ
1	0.203	Federal Signal Corp.	176	99	479
2	0.304	Sturm Ruger & Co.	176	58	339
3	0.385	Crown Cork & Seal Inc.	176	39	224
4	0.463	Rust Intl., Inc.	176	57	216
5	0.548	Bethlehem Steel Corp.	176	40	187
6	0.636	Piccadilly Cafeteria	176	42	180
7	0.744	PSI Resources Inc.	176	45	193
8	0.889	Pilgrim's Pride Corp.	176	54	206
9	1.148	Penn Cent Corp.	176	90	186
10	13.100	Martech USA Inc.	176	157	302

The 1,760 companies on the New York Stock Exchange are divided into 10 equal groups (deciles) based on book-to-market ratios. American Stock Exchange and NASDAQ issues are added to the NYSE decile groupings.

FIGURE 9–3
Historical Returns, 1964–94

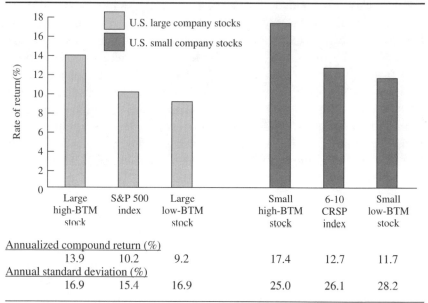

	Large high-BTM stock	S&P 500 index	Large low-BTM stock	Small high-BTM stock	6-10 CRSP index	Small low-BTM stock
Annualized compound return (%)	13.9	10.2	9.2	17.4	12.7	11.7
Annual standard deviation (%)	16.9	15.4	16.9	25.0	26.1	28.2

Source: Data courtesy Fama and French. Value and growth include hold ranges and estimated trading costs. April 1993–Present: Dimensional's Value Mutual Fund Portfolios, net of all fees.

This relatively low BTM ratio would be expected, since the S&P 500 index is weighted. Those companies that have higher market capitalizations are weighted more heavily in the composition of the index.

In Figure 9–3, Fama and French simulated the performance of both high-BTM stocks and low-BTM stocks for both large and small companies. Large company stocks were defined as those stocks in the 1st through 5th deciles based on market capitalization. Small company stocks were defined as those in the 6th through 10th, based on market capitalization. The benchmark portfolio for large companies was the S&P 500. The benchmark for small company stocks was the Center for Research in Securities Prices (CRSP) index (6th through 10th deciles).

Fama and French determined that risk, as measured by standard deviation, is roughly the same for all stocks in a given size category, whatever their BTM ratios. However, they found that the high-BTM stocks produced a higher average annual return. In fact, high-BTM stocks as a group produced greater than a 4 percent higher return with the same standard deviation as the low-BTM stocks. In Figure 9–3, large high-BTM stocks outperform large low-BTM stocks by 4.7 percent (13.9% less 9.2%). The specific risk of owning one of the high-BTM stocks is significant. However, owning all of the high-BTM stocks in a broad asset class is similar in risk to owning all the stocks in the market. Thus, we can expect higher returns at similar levels of market risk.

THE INTERNATIONAL THREE-FACTOR MODEL

Does the three-factor market work internationally? Another recent study by Carlo Capaul and Ian Rowley, conducted in conjunction with Stanford University's William Sharpe, both supported and supplemented Fama and French's findings.[3] Their research showed that an international high-BTM stock portfolio not only outperformed the recognized global indexes, but the excess returns were also greater on average than those found in the United States. These excess returns, combined with the low correlation of returns between countries, allow for lower risk.

FIGURE 9–4
Historical Returns, 1975–92

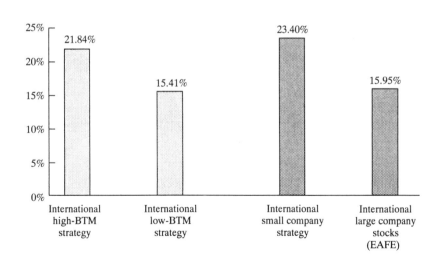

Building an international asset class high-BTM portfolio presents many challenges. First, investors have to face the cost of doing business overseas, as we discussed in Chapter Seven. However, that can be partly overcome through the wise use of institutional asset class funds. But how do investors cope with the varying accounting rules in the rest of the world? The answer is quite simple: We are interested in capturing the relative BTM risk factor in each country and do not have to compare accounting standards between countries. The same screening process we discussed for the United States is used for each country.

Fama and French went on to calculate the relative performance of an international high-BTM asset class portfolio against both Morgan Stanley's EAFE Index and a low-BTM portfolio (see Figure 9–4). The results were even more dramatic than the comparison with U.S. assets. The difference in returns between high- and low-BTM portfolios was over 600 basis points. The difference in returns between high-BTM portfolios and the EAFE Index was almost 500 basis points. This result is just too huge for us to ignore.

WHY THIS EXCESS PERFORMANCE?

High book-to-market ratios mean distress. The market sets a low market price relative to the company's book value and that results in a high BTM to compensate for the risk. There are at least two risks associated with the high-BTM effect. One is psychic risk when dealing with "ugly" stocks that don't perform—and you've got to take responsibility for what turns out to be "poor judgment." Ugly stocks are companies in distress. People who manage investment portfolios have trouble explaining to their boards of directors why they're holding such ugly stocks. Suppose you purchase IBM, for example. IBM does okay. Well, that's fine; no big deal. Now suppose IBM does poorly during that quarter. You bought IBM because it's a high-BTM stock. It does poorly. Now your portfolio is in trouble and you've got to explain your strategy to your board of directors. They're going to look over your shoulder and say, "How could you be such a fool as to buy IBM? Everybody knew IBM was in trouble." That's the psychic risk—that you'll be in the hot seat.

Investors who aren't accountable to a board of directors, who don't have anybody looking over their shoulders, don't have to deal with psychic risk. It is their money, and no one is pointing a finger at them, magnifying their regret. They don't have any more psychic risk with IBM than they do with Microsoft.

The second risk of the high-BTM effect is based on Merton Miller's work regarding the cost of capital. High-BTM stocks have poor earning prospects. Companies with poor earning prospects have a higher cost of capital than companies with great earning prospects. Companies that are doing poorly pay a higher rate to borrow money than companies that are doing well. In the equity market, this translates into a higher expected rate of return on equity capital for investors who provide that capital.

It is very hard to stay on track with the tremendous amount of misinformation present. Often, things are not as they appear. For all investors, a written investment plan that makes sure they stay on track adds substantial value. In the next chapter, you will learn how to put your own investment plan together.

ENDNOTES

[1]Fama, Eugene F., and Kenneth R. French, "The Cross-Section of Expected Stock Returns," *Journal of Finance* (June 1992), pp. 427–65.

[2]Clayton, Michele, "In Search of Excellence: The Investor's Viewpoint." *Financial Analysts Journal* (June 1987).

[3]Capaul, Carlo; Ian Rowley; and William F. Sharpe, "International Value and Growth Stock Returns," *Financial Analysts Journal* (January–February 1993), pp. 27–36.

Chapter Ten

The Working Document–Your Investment Policy Statement

I n this chapter you will learn how to clearly articulate your own personal investment program in a workable strategy that you can implement in both good and bad markets. You might compare this to a business plan; very few successful businesses have started and succeeded without one. Institutional investors call these written investment plans "investment policy statements." You can use the same technique. We feel that it is the critical first step, and we have prepared one with each of our clients, without exception.

An investment policy statement defines the investor's financial objectives, the amount of funds available for investment, the investment methodology, and the strategy that will be used to reach those objectives. This statement matches an individual investor's objectives to their goals and helps identify risk-tolerance levels.

A written investment policy statement enables you to clearly communicate your long-term goals and objectives to your advisor—or it will serve as a guideline if you are implementing the investment strategy on your own. The written policy statement helps you maintain a sound long-term plan, even while short-term market movements cause you to second-guess whether what you learned works.

We believe all investors should have an investment policy statement that outlines their goals and how their money will be invested to reach those goals. Here's why: Investors can get caught up in the emotions of the day. It's only through long-term planning that they are going to be successful and not fall back into old habits. In the heat of a market downturn, it is critical to have a strategy that you have thought out well ahead of time.

Creating an investment policy statement embodies the essence of the financial planning process: assessing where you are now and where you want to go and developing a strategy for getting there. Having and using this policy statement compels you to become more disciplined and systematic, thus increasing the probability of satisfying your investment goals. In addition, if you are a trustee, the development and use of a written investment policy statement will go a long way toward ensuring that you meet any fiduciary responsibilities.

EIGHT STEPS TO ESTABLISHING AN INVESTMENT POLICY

1. Set your long-term goals and objectives clearly and concisely. Long-term goals can be anything from early retirement to purchasing a new home. One of the most common goals we have found among our clients is financial independence. What that often means to our clients is that their investment portfolio alone will provide them with the income necessary to maintain their quality of life. This is just as important for clients who are still working as for those who are already retired.

2. Define the level of risk you are willing to accept. Along the road to reaching your financial goals, there are going to be bumps caused by downturns in various markets. It is important for you to understand the amount of risk you're willing to tolerate during the investment period. In designing your portfolio, you must determine the absolute maximum loss you're willing to accept in any one-year period without terminating your investment program. No one can predict market movements, and you have to be in a position to weather any storm.

As we stated in Chapter Eight, the best way to determine the level of risk in a portfolio is to look at its performance during 1973 and 1974. Those years experienced the worst financial recession since World War II. Investors should be honest with themselves. The next two years might be similar. There is a 5 percent probability that in the next year we will experience a similar downturn. You probably remember waiting in line for gas in 1973–74. The S&P 500 index lost 37.2 percent and small company stocks lost 56.5 percent in those years. Most investors would have a hard time maintaining a long-term perspective and staying with the program.

Before you invest, you should require from your financial advisor an analysis of how your portfolio would have performed during 1973–74. In the Appendix, simulated model-portfolio returns for each year from 1972 to 1994 are illustrated to assist you in this process. Choose the portfolio with which you would have been comfortable. If you would have closed your account because of that downturn, you are taking too much risk and should consider the lower-risk model portfolio. Investments tend to be cyclical and no one can predict their performance in the short term. The best-performing year for both the S&P 500 index and small company stocks was 1975, when they earned 37.2 percent and 65.7 percent, respectively.

3. Establish the expected time horizon for your investment. Each investor has to determine the investment period for his or her capital. The minimum expected investment period must be at least five years for any portfolio containing equity securities. For any portfolio with less than a five-year time horizon, the portfolio should be made up predominantly of fixed investments. This five-year minimum investment period is critical. The investment process must be viewed as a long-term plan for achieving the desired results. One-year volatility can be significant for many equity asset classes, as you can see in the appendix. However, over a five-year period, the range of returns is greatly reduced.

FIGURE 10–1
Returns for the Conservative Model Portfolio, 1972–94

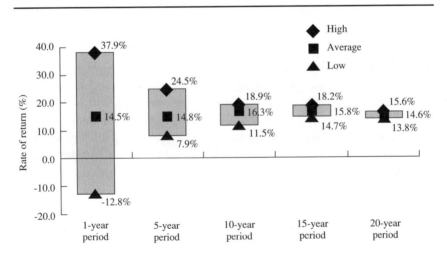

As Figure 10–1 indicates, if you're planning to invest for a lifetime, the range of returns of a model portfolio approaches zero.

4. Determine the rate of return objective. Even sophisticated investors tend to focus on their rate of return objectives rather than risk. The rate of return is going to be a direct result of your willingness to take risk and your search for the long-term nature of your objectives. In getting started, you should write down a range of returns that would be acceptable. In Chapter Eight we listed the specific expected return profile of each asset class. We have shown them for each optimized model portfolio in Table 10–1. If you are doing this on your own, you can use these ranges of returns for each risk level as the framework to determine your return expectation for your portfolio as well as its component asset classes.

TABLE 10–1
Expected Returns for Model Portfolios

Model Portfolio	Expected Returns %
Defensive	10.2
Conservative	12.4
Moderate	14.1
Aggressive	15.7

Your range should be consistent with the weighted-average expected rate of return of your portfolio asset classes over the last 20 years. Don't just look at the last 5 years; that is likely to be an unusual period. You will also want to examine some difficult market periods, such as the 1973–74 time frame, to see if you can stay the course.

5. Select the asset classes to be utilized to build your portfolio. In Chapters Six and Seven, we examined the institutional and retail asset class mutual funds available to you. List all the different asset classes that you might want to consider in your portfolio. You may be surprised to find differences between what you've been using in the past and what you should be using.

6. Document the investment methodology to be utilized in managing your portfolio. As we discussed in Chapter Three, there are three basic investment methodologies: security selection, market timing, and Asset Class Investing. The only proven methodology for the prudent investor to use is Asset Class Investing.

7. Establish a strategic implementation plan. Once you've identified the first six components of your investment policy, you need to determine how you're going to allocate your capital to each asset class. In Chapter Eight we referred to the mathematical techniques that can be used in determining your optimal portfolio, which falls on the efficient frontier. Those investors without a strong math background may want to use one of our model portfolios.

8. Establish the means for making periodic adjustments to your portfolio as needed. The investment policy statement creates a benchmark for reviewing investment portfolio performance. If goals and objectives have been clearly defined, it becomes much easier to determine how the portfolio is performing relative to these goals and objectives.

Creating an investment roadmap is an essential step for investors in successfully managing their own expectations. To be a successful investor, you must take full responsibility for your investment portfolio decisions. Being responsible, however, does not mean that you need to become a bona fide expert in portfolio theory and make all the difficult asset-allocation decisions yourself. Instead, you need to familiarize yourself sufficiently with the operating rules contained within this book and determine whether you should manage your portfolio on your own or seek a competent investment advisor to assist you in the implementation of your plan. The written policy statement will enable you to define your investment expectations better and will allow you to decide how best to implement your asset class portfolio. If you hire an investment advisor, you will be better able to supervise your advisor.

PRUDENT INVESTOR GUIDELINES

Most individual investors are not trustees who are subject to the following guidelines. If you are not a fiduciary, you may want to jump ahead to the next chapter where we will discuss how to stay on track with your new asset class portfolio. However, if you are a trustee, it is important that you understand your responsibilities and how Asset Class Investing can help you fulfill your fiduciary obligations.

The written investment policy statement creates a road map for fiduciaries to meet the legal requirements in the "prudent investor" rules. The written plan also provides standards against which the trustee can be judged. The written investment policy statement must be clear and specific enough to be a working document. Broad-based generalities will not serve as investment objectives. Being specific is the key to providing a proper, working investment plan.

The American Law Institute Restatement of the Law Third, Prudent Investor Rules, instructs trustees and courts that:

- Sound diversification is fundamental to risk management and is therefore ordinarily required of trustees.
- Risk and returns are so directly related that trustees have a duty to analyze and make conscious decisions concerning the level of risk appropriate for the purposes, requirements, and circumstances of the trust.
- Trustees have a duty to avoid fees, transaction costs, and other expenses that are not justified by the needs and realistic objectives of the trust's investment program.
- The fiduciary duty of impartiality requires a balancing of current income and the protection of purchasing power.
- Trustees may have the duty as well as the authority to delegate as prudent investors would.

The prudent investor rules are becoming prudent investor laws in many states. We feel that it is critical to follow these guidelines and prepare an investment policy statement that will protect you and your family.

Chapter Eleven

Staying on Track—The Source of Winning Results

W ith all the distractions you are going to face, it is going to be easy for you to get sidetracked. With stockbrokers calling you at home with their latest, hottest investment product; the investment magazine headlines promising overnight investment success; and the television experts pitching their investment secrets, you are going to second-guess your investment strategy, Asset Class Investing.

When your portfolio returns are not steady, the naysayers will try to play to your emotions. You must stay the course to reach your goals. It is because returns are not linear that you can make higher returns. If returns were perfectly linear, then many fixed-income investors would reposition their investments to take advantage. This would bring market returns down substantially to fixed-income levels.

You must have reasonable expectations for the short term. Viewing the last 69 years of stock market performance will help you better understand what you might expect. During the period from January 1926 through December 1994, an investor would have had to earn a 3.1 percent average return per year just to keep pace with inflation. On average, it would take $8.38 today to buy the same goods that $1 bought in 1926. Most investors want, at minimum, to set a goal of maintaining their purchasing power.

For maintaining purchasing power, stock market investing has been very effective over the long term. Standard & Poor's 500 index grew at an average rate of 10.2 percent per year from 1926 to 1994. One dollar invested in stocks in the S&P 500 would have grown to $811 over this time period. Even after considering income taxes and the spending of dividend income, common stock investments kept pace with inflation. Higher expected total returns are the reason that we invest in equities.

The S&P 500 index's returns include a risk premium over Treasury bills to compensate for the additional risk investors assume in the stock market. This risk premium is not a constant each month or quarter. If the best-performing month for the S&P 500 during each calendar year were removed from the performance statistics, we would find that returns dropped to a meager 1.2 percent per year. Your account would have grown to only $2.32—a great deal less than $811, if all months were included. Over 90 percent of the gain recorded each year has been concentrated in a single, 30-day period of time. We can expect this relationship to continue, with only one or two of the four quarterly reviews each calendar year resulting in positive returns on average. The other two or three quarters will be flat or down. While this prospect seems unexciting, it's important, because it is only through a patient, long-term perspective that you will realize your financial goals.

Small company stocks have enjoyed better long-term performance than large company stocks, due to their higher risk. As indicated in Figure 11–1, the small company stocks have grown at an average annual rate of 11.97 percent over this 69-year period. Although these stocks are more volatile by nature than the large company stocks, the rewards have justified the higher risk. One dollar invested in small company stocks at the beginning of 1926 would have grown to $2,440.21 by the end of 1994. Missing the best-performing month in each calendar year would have reduced the total return to –2.6 percent. The account would have fallen from $1.00 to a mere 16¢, versus $2,440.21 if all months had been counted.

FIGURE 11–1
Growth of $1, January 1926 through December 1994

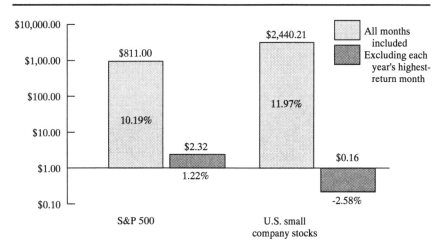

The model portfolios we designed in Chapter Eight minimize the equity risk by selecting among four major equity classes: (1) U.S. large company stocks; (2) U.S. small company stocks; (3) international large company stocks; and (4) international small company stocks. These four equity asset classes represent over 5,000 different stock positions in 14 different countries. This extremely broad diversification, combined with a disciplined, long-term perspective, will increase the likelihood that you will successfully reach your financial goals. Along the way, short-term results will vary. However, you can expect the long-term results to maintain a level of consistency that will allow you to stay the charted course.

To further understand how each individual model portfolio will perform, we've simulated their returns on a quarter-by-quarter basis from January 1972 to December 1994, a 23-year period. The 1970s was a decade of poor market performance, with the 1973–74 period being the worst bear market since World War II. During the 1980s, the market rallied sharply to set many record highs and generate steady profits for equity investors. So the 23-year period from 1972 through 1994 includes enough market fluctuations to be a good model upon which to set your future expectations.

FIGURE 11–2
Moderate Portfolio Quarterly Performance, January 1972 to December 1994

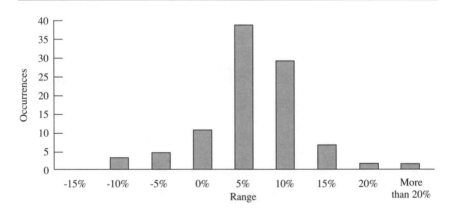

First, let's review the most popular model portfolio among our clients, the Moderate portfolio. Figure 11–2 simulates the performance for the Moderate portfolio on a quarter-by-quarter basis. For each range of returns, we graph the frequency of its occurrence during this 23-year period. Figure 11–2 indicates that 3 of the 92 quarters being measured would have shown losses of 10 to 15 percent. On the upside, 1 of the 92 quarters would have realized a gain that exceeded 20 percent. More than 80 percent of the quarters produced positive investment results, while less than 20 percent of the quarters had negative results. The overall simulated performance during this 23-year period of ups and downs was a very respectable 15.8 percent annual compound rate of return.

FIGURE 11–3
Conservative Portfolio Quarterly Performance, January 1972 to December 1994

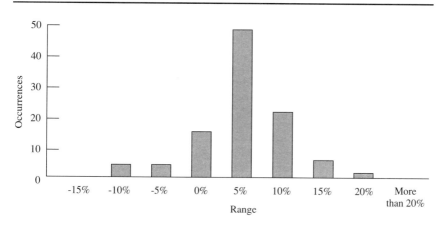

Figures 11–3 and 11–4 show the distributions of simulated quarterly performance for the Conservative and Aggressive portfolios. The charts give us a good illustration of the risk/reward relationships within these portfolios. As we increase our risk tolerances from conservative to moderate to aggressive, we see an increased volatility in the portfolios. Along with the increased volatility comes an increasing expected rate of return, ranging from 14.1 percent for the Conservative portfolio to 17.5 percent for the Aggressive portfolio.

Figure 11–5 illustrates the results of lowering the equity component to 25 percent of your portfolio. The Defensive portfolio's distribution of simulated quarterly performance is centered around the mean. For this lower volatility you would have experienced lower returns of 10.2 percent.

FIGURE 11–4

Aggressive Portfolio Quarterly Performance, January 1972 to December 1994

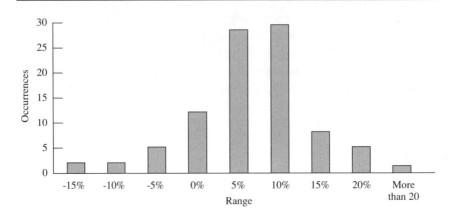

FIGURE 11–5

Defensive Portfolio Quarterly Performance, January 1972 to December 1994

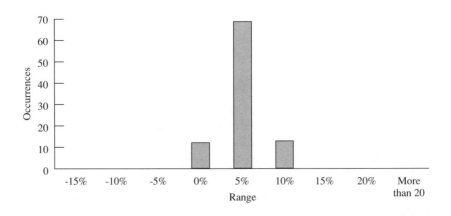

In order to gain these high rates of return during the past 23 years, it was necessary to invest in the stock market. If an investor had merely purchased certificates of deposit (CDs) and bonds, performance would have been only slightly better than the rate of inflation for this same period. The price we must pay for improved investment portfolio performance is an increase in overall portfolio volatility. The volatility becomes less significant the longer the investment time horizon.

Figures 11–2 through 11–5 show that not every quarter has a positive return. In fact, we should realistically expect only one of every four quarters to show significant net gains. In addition, 3 of the last 23 years showed annual losses in our simulation. Assuming that history repeats itself, asset class investors will need to remain disciplined and not give into emotion when the market has its normal up and down cycles.

THE FOUR STEPS IN QUARTERLY REVIEWS

To deal with these ups and downs, you need a formal, quarterly review procedure to make sure you are staying on track. In Figure 11–6, we have illustrated the four steps that we use each quarter.

FIGURE 11–6
The Four Steps in Quarterly Reviews

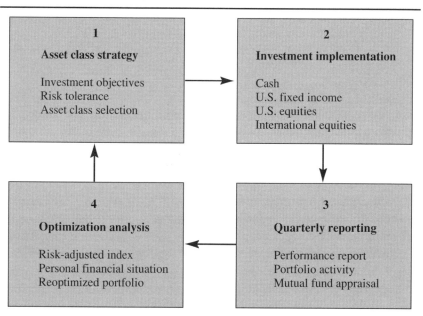

Step 1: Asset Class Strategy

The first step is to establish your asset class strategy. You complete this step through your written investment policy statement, as we discussed in Chapter Ten. At a minimum, you must have clear investment objectives, determine your risk tolerance, and identify your asset class selections for inclusion in your portfolio. Each quarter, you should review your portfolio to make sure that none of your investment guidelines have changed.

Step 2: Investment Implementation

Once your asset strategy is developed, you are ready to implement your investment program. You have three key questions to ask yourself.

1. Do you work with an investment advisor? If so, see Chapter Fourteen for advice on selecting an investment advisor.
2. Do you work directly with the mutual fund provider or with a broker/dealer who handles many mutual fund families? If you are working with a broker/dealer who provides a mutual fund marketplace, you would want to choose from their list.
3. Which specific asset class mutual funds will you select? To assist you in this process, see Chapter Six, which includes a list of currently available mutual funds, and Chapter Seven.

Step 3: Quarterly Reporting

Each calendar quarter, you should review your account. If you are working with an investment advisor, his or her report should clearly determine exactly how the account has performed, both for the portfolio as a whole and for each individual asset class. The portfolio activity should also be included in this report.

If you are working on your own, you will be responsible for reviewing the account statements and calculating the quarterly performance in each of the asset classes. Compare these reports with the expectations in your investment policy statement to make sure you stay on track. If the performance is not consistent with the policy statement, there is a need for immediate change. You should be just as concerned with overperformance of expectations as with underperformance. If one of your asset class mutual funds is outside your expectations, it is likely that it is using an active management strategy and should be replaced.

Step 4: Optimization Analysis

In our firm we evaluate the efficiency of our clients' portfolios each quarter. Efficiency is measured by a risk-adjusted return index. This index measures the relative trade-off an investor is willing to accept in risk for an incremental increase in expected rate of return. "Fine-tuning" trades are made when the account's risk-adjusted return index can be improved through reoptimization. Trading costs are considered. If you are implementing the asset class strategy on your own, rebalancing to the original model portfolio allocation should be done quarterly. The transaction costs associated with rebalancing should be considered before executing any trades. For portfolios of less than $50,000, you should rebalance annually.

DISCIPLINE VERSUS THE PURSUIT OF THE BEST-PERFORMING MUTUAL FUNDS

The secret to Asset Class Investing is having the discipline to stay on track. If you are confident, maintaining a disciplined approach is not hard to do. If you lose this discipline, you're in for another ride on the emotional roller coaster. Only a thoughtful understanding of Asset Class Investing will provide the foundation for discipline and keep you on track. Do not revert to trying to pick the top mutual fund of the year. It is impossible.

In Table 11–1, we have tracked how the top 10 funds each year did in subsequent years. Examine the chart and you will see that many "name-brand" mutual funds are in the top 10. However, look where they are in the next few years. Self-proclaimed investment experts will be telling you to get off course and choose your mutual fund by its track record. So widespread is the investing public's belief in track records that many magazines, newspapers, and professional rating services that publish their recommendations utilize the funds' track records as their primary means of selection. They use the media to draw attention to the successful performance of the top mutual funds for the year out of self-interest. You must ignore the call. It is only through the consistency of Asset Class Investing that you can enjoy the highest likelihood of financial success.

TABLE 11–1
Top 10 Mutual Funds Ranking, 1985–94

	1985	1986	1987	1988	1989	1990	1991	1992	1993	1994
Total Funds	*765*	*969*	*1,230*	*1,555*	*1,773*	*1,925*	*2,216*	*2,589*	*3,339*	*4,580*
1985										
Fidelity Overseas	1	6	52	1,111	745	1,449	2,071	2,538	123	526
Fidelity OTC Portfolio	2	732	544	121	213	1,336	161	249	2,551	1,805
Paine Webber Atlas: Gl Gro/A	3	39	195	211	618	1,505	2,034	2,505	109	4,429
Putnam Global Growth/A	4	43	178	1,039	426	1,577	1,058	2,287	230	1,129
Alliance Int'l/A	5	30	1,080	21	233	1,858	2,096	2,463	303	133
Int'l Srs: Int'l Equity/A	6	14	570	362	684	1,660	2,101	2,465	241	702
Fidelity Select: Health Care	7	125	794	1,060	39	4	14	2,569	3,200	13
Fidelity Select: Leisure	8	467	231	70	194	1,873	480	203	127	3,556
Kemper Int'l	9	29	201	304	673	1,499	2,047	2,441	162	2,399
Twentieth Century: Giftrust	10	72	144	805	15	1,811	12	147	239	41
1986										
Merrill Pacific Fund/A		1	111	17	847	1,539	1,105	2,507	184	290
Japan Fund		2	19	233	106	1,797	2,166	2,367	379	39
Nomura Pacific Basin		3	18	350	500	1,766	1,711	2,549	119	1,364
INVESCO Int'l: Pacific Basin		4	118	110	607	1,889	1,477	2,556	105	184
GT Global Pacific Growth/A		5	229	109	19	1,640	1,489	2,488	54	4,538
Fidelity Overseas		6	52	1,111	745	1,449	2,071	2,538	123	526
Schroder Capital: Int'l Equity		7	358	228	532	1,655	2,153	2,426	95	941
T Rowe Price Int'l Stock		8	156	280	456	1,561	1,177	2,413	121	1,106
GT Japan Growth/A		9	4	148	4	1,912	2,191	2,578	198	113
Fidelity Destiny Plan II		10	182	123	347	1,197	273	229	308	193
1987										
DFA: Japanese Small Co			1	23	68	1,918	2,117	2,582	1,049	3
Oppenheimer Gold & Special Minerals			2	1,100	118	1,903	2,181	2,523	51	3,250
IDS Precious Metals			3	1,540	706	1,884	2,195	2,508	21	4,201
GT Japan Growth/A			4	148	4	1,912	2,191	2,578	198	113
DFA: UK Small Co Portfolio			5	1,281	1,766	1,451	1,300	2,561	255	186
Franklin Gold			6	1,534	43	1,844	2,142	2,576	35	2,738
Van Eck: Gold Resources			7	1,550	659	1,901	2,197	2,437	27	4,489
Lexington Goldfund			8	1,542	450	1,857	2,204	2,577	17	3,699
Keystone Precious Metals Holdings			9	1,543	425	1,900	2,081	2,557	6	4,448
Fidelity Select: American Gold			10	1,537	536	1,817	2,203	2,399	26	4,484
1988										
Kaufmann Fund				1	20	1,415	16	418	645	71
Sun America Eq: Small Co				2	486	1,904	118	102	1,086	182
Columbia Special				3	170	1,687	147	297	496	384
Parnassus Fund				4	1,713	1,863	132	11	702	46
Vista: Growth and Income/A				5	8	1,042	90	243	1,332	2,132
Ariel Growth				6	400	1,793	485	573	2,495	2,501
Gabelli Growth				7	54	1,172	442	2,017	1,892	2,103
Fidelity Select: Retailing				8	239	1,349	39	60	1,318	2,877
Fidelity Select: Transport				9	271	1,866	126	46	273	234
Harbor: Int'l				10	92	1,600	929	2,306	96	148

TABLE 11–1 *(continued)*
Top 10 Mutual Funds Ranking, 1985–94

	1985	1986	1987	1988	1989	1990	1991	1992	1993	1994
Total Funds	*765*	*969*	*1,230*	*1,555*	*1,773*	*1,925*	*2,216*	*2,589*	*3,339*	*4,580*
1989										
United Services: Gold Shares					1	1,919	2,212	2,588	2	1,787
Alger: Small Capital					2	468	122	2,070	1,385	2,693
Lexington Strategic Investments					3	1,924	2,215	2,589	1	51
GT Japan Growth/A					4	1,912	2,191	2,578	198	113
INVESCO Strategic: Health Sciences					5	3	6	2,559	3,335	599
Fidelity Select: Energy Services					6	957	2,216	2,114	486	715
Fidelity Select: Medical					7	20	17	2,552	2,960	16
Vista: Growth and Income/A					8	1,042	90	243	1,332	2,132
GT America Growth/A					9	1,493	998	17	2,549	27
Twentieth Century: Vista					10	1,780	25	2,360	2,970	183
1990										
Fidelity Select: Biotech						1	3	2,526	3,257	4,526
Fidelity Sterling Performance						2	2,,135	2,542	3,206	61
INVESCO Strategic: Health Sciences						3	6	2,559	3,335	599
Fidelity Select: Health Care						4	14	2,569	3,200	13
Kemper Global Income						5	1833	2,352	2,140	1,304
Equity Strategies						6	1,579	2,174	643	Liquidated 5/94
Fidelity D-Mark Performance Portfolio						7	2,140	2,260	3,296	24
Scudder Global: Int'l Bond						8	900	1,286	817	4,037
Phoenix Multi: Capital Appreciation						9	172	1,116	2,162	2,324
Franklin Templeton Global: Hard Currency						10	2,079	2,199	3,047	30
1991										
Oppenheimer Global Emerging Growth							1	2,580	3,286	4,568
CGM Capital Development							2	161	283	4,558
Fidelity Select: Biotech							3	2,526	3,257	4,526
Montgomery Small Capital							4	651	363	4,260
American Heritage							5	122	114	4,576
INVESCO Strategic: Health Sciences							6	2,559	3,335	599
Berger One Hundred Fund							7	978	469	3,509
United New Concepts							8	2,014	2,022	52
MFS Emerging Growth/B							9	397	371	220
Oberwise Emerging Growth							10	296	2,267	2,185
1992										
Fidelity Select: Home Finance								1	298	343
Oakmark Fund								2	260	278
Fidelity Select: Regional Bank								3	1,915	779
J Hancock Freedom: Regional Bank/B								4	505	921
Fidelity Select: Financial Services								5	681	2,236
Heartland Group: Value								6	600	464
Skyline: Special Equity								7	404	1,221
Fidelity Select: Automotive								8	168	4,432
PaineWebber Regional Financial Growth/A								9	2,188	1,102
PaineWebber Regional Financial Growth/B								10	2,306	1,326

TABLE 11–1 *(continued)*
Top 10 Mutual Funds Ranking, 1985–94

	1985	1986	1987	1988	1989	1990	1991	1992	1993	1994
Total Funds	*765*	*969*	*1,230*	*1,555*	*1,773*	*1,925*	*2,216*	*2,589*	*3,339*	*4,580*
1993										
Lexington Strategic Investments									1	51
United Services: Gold Shares									2	1,787
Van Eck: Int'l Investors									3	1,191
Fidelity Select: Precious Metals									4	1,211
Morgan Stanley Instit: Asian Equity									5	4,491
Keystone Precious Metals Holdings									6	4,448
Blanchard Precious Metals									7	4,479
Excel Midas Gold Shares									8	4,512
Dean Witter Pacific Growth									9	4,518
Vanquard Specialized: Gold & Precious Metals									10	3,050
1994										
Seligman Commun & Info/A										1
Seligman Commun & Info/D										2
DFA: Japanese Small Co										3
Govett: Smaller Companies										4
Alliance Technology/A										5
Alliance Technology/C										6
Alliance Technology/B										7
Merrill Technology/A										8
Merrill Technology/B										9
Capstone Int'l: Nikko Japan										10

Source: All data taken from Alexander Steele's software <u>Mutual Fund Expert</u>, Copyright 1992-94. "December 30, 1994, Equity/Fixed Data Base". (View used: Funds Only—No Indexes or Averages). Unfortunately, funds that did not survive the whole period shown above dropped out of the database, as if they never existed.

Let's go back to where we started and test our investment strategy. In Chapter Two we examined the five needs of all investors. We found these needs to be consistent for everyone and paramount to any successful investment program. Beginning with Chapter Three and proceeding through Chapter Eleven, we proved that Asset Class Investing is the only viable solution to today's investment challenges. Now, in Chapter Twelve, we will close the loop and prove that Asset Class Investing does meet all five investor needs. Then we will be ready to build and implement your portfolio.

Chapter Twelve

Does Asset Class Investing Meet Investor Needs?

I n this chapter, we'll assess whether Asset Class Investing has met the five basic needs that most investors share, as we outlined in Chapter Two. One by one, we will test the concepts of Asset Class Investing and determine if it is truly the logical way to meet these needs. Then, as a prudent investor, you will have the confidence necessary to develop and implement your own "beat the market" portfolio, as outlined in the next chapter.

INVESTOR NEED 1: DOES ASSET CLASS INVESTING REDUCE RISK?

While risk cannot be eliminated from the equity market, it can be effectively controlled utilizing Asset Class Investing. Not only do these strategies reduce risk, they allow you the opportunity to select your specific level of risk quantitatively. This is accomplished through a technique we discussed in Chapter Four, called dissimilar price movement diversification. As we pointed out, this is done by assembling a portfolio of dissimilar asset classes. These asset classes have low historical correlations with each other. This means that the dissimilar asset classes within a portfolio will tend to move in different cycles. By investing in these equity and fixed-income asset classes, an investor can increase diversification, decrease risk, and increase profit—the foundation of Asset Class Investing. No other method of investing allows the investor to design a portfolio so concisely to a personal level of risk. This method's success is due to the exacting construction of each asset class.

A proliferation of different asset class studies has produced a tremendous amount of data concerning how each asset class has performed over time. This data allows investors to identify which asset classes exhibit dissimilar prices. With dissimilar asset classes, one class may move up, a second down, while a third has no movement at all. The movements of these different asset classes therefore tend to lessen short-term volatility, while the expected rate of return is simply the weighted-average return. The overall portfolio has a much lower volatility.

Using dissimilar-price-movement diversification has another advantage. It enables the investor to take advantage of relatively high-risk, high-return asset classes within a conservative portfolio. These asset classes can be included within a portfolio if they have low correlation coefficients.

Each of the model portfolios has less risk than the market portfolio, as illustrated in Table 12–1.

TABLE 12–1
Risk of Selected Indexes and Portfolios

Index/Portfolio	Annual Standard Deviation %
Defensive	5.1
Conservative	8.6
Moderate	11.6
Aggressive	14.1
S&P 500	15.7

INVESTOR NEED 2: DOES ASSET CLASS INVESTING INCREASE RETURNS?

All investors have the same goal: to maximize returns with the least amount of risk. So how does Asset Class Investing maximize your return on investment? In Chapter Five, we demonstrated that two portfolios with the same average rate of return may have different compound rates of return. The portfolio with the lower volatility will always have the higher compound rate of return. Compound returns build wealth. Asset class portfolios are built to realize this higher rate of return by lowering volatility through their use of dissimilar price movements. The straighter the path, the sooner you will get there. Return is enhanced.

In addition, by positioning your portfolio to stay invested for the long term, you will participate in the market's wealth creation without all the costs associated with active management. Each company acts in its own, enlightened self-interest to maximize its own company's stock value. Not all will be successful. Many will. Your broad diversification through asset classes will enhance your returns by capturing the market effect.

Each of the asset class model portfolios has returns greater than the market portfolio, as illustrated in Figure 12–1.

FIGURE 12–1
Growth of $1, January 1973 through December 1994

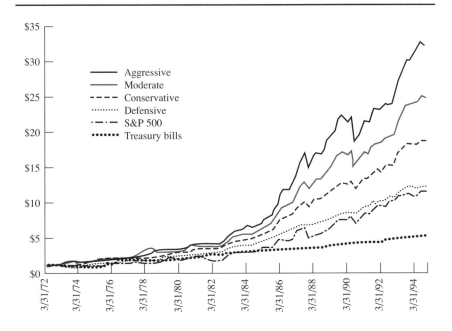

INVESTOR NEED 3: DOES ASSET CLASS INVESTING HELP INVESTORS REACH THEIR FINANCIAL GOALS?

In Chapter Ten, we discussed the importance of developing your own investment policy statement—knowing where you are now, where you want to go, and how you are going to get there. In any business, you need to take a step back to look at the larger picture before you get started.

Most businesses have failed due to poor planning. Even for such a seemingly simple task as planting a row of crops, you need a benchmark. Every farmer knows he can't plow straight by looking at where he is now. He has to plant a stake out ahead of his field and then keep his eye on the stake. If you are going to follow a straight path to achieve your financial goals, you also need to drive a stake far enough in the future to stay on course. No other investment strategy allows you to design and follow such a concise course.

Before investors implement their Asset Class Investing portfolios, they must have written their investment policy statements to assure that they can stay on course. In Chapter Ten, we have provided a step-by-step approach to constructing your own investment policy statement. But creating it is not enough. Each quarter, you should compare benchmarks with realized performance to keep on track. It is through this disciplined approach that your goals can be realized.

How can you set this diversification strategy in motion and assure yourself that you will have the discipline necessary to stay the course? The key is to develop a written investment policy statement outlining a disciplined plan that will shield you from the day-to-day sensationalism sponsored by the media. There will be constant temptation, particularly if you read the financial tabloids, to second-guess the strategy in your plan. You will have to fight the urge to try the hottest new mutual fund or Wall Street's "investment of the day." Executing a disciplined investment plan in this environment may be easier said than done.

The customized investment policy statement that you develop on your own, or jointly with your financial advisor, serves as a road map. It will help you ignore the messages in magazines or your local newspaper that spread panic, such as "Markets reach new highs. Time to run for the cover of your money market fund." Again, you will also be spared from the temptation to continually switch your funds to the latest investments touted daily in full-page ads. You have to have a plan to meet your objectives.

INVESTOR NEED 4: DOES ASSET CLASS INVESTING PROVIDE A DEPENDABLE INCOME STREAM?

Let's examine the Conservative model portfolio and see if it would have provided a dependable income stream. Reviewing the 23-year period from January 1, 1972, through December 31, 1994, indicates that U.S.

Treasury bills earned an average annual compound rate of return of 7.2 percent. During this same period, Standard and Poor's 500 index earned 11.1 percent, and the simulated return for the Conservative portfolio was 14.1 percent. These percentages would lead us to believe that the safest way to invest for a steady income and still have our investment portfolio grow would be by utilizing the Conservative model portfolio, with the S&P 500 a close second and Treasury bills far behind.

We have assumed that $100,000 was invested in each of three investment alternatives (Treasury bills, S&P 500, and the Conservative model portfolio) and $2,000 per quarter was arbitrarily withdrawn from each investment. This withdrawal rate, at 8 percent of your original investment, seems reasonable. What were the results? They can be seen in Figure 12–2.

FIGURE 12–2
Conservative Portfolio vs. S&P 500 and Treasury Bills
(Less Quarterly Income of $2,000), 1972–94

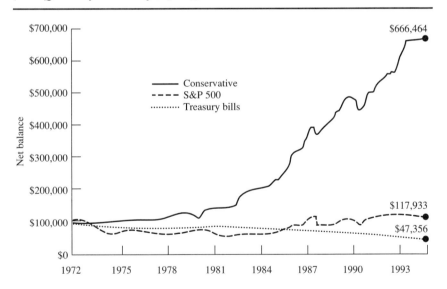

The chart shows quite graphically that Treasury bills present the greatest problem for an income investor. Historically, they have failed to earn a high enough rate to pay out 8 percent per year. The initial investment of $100,000 fell to $47,356, and this is before adjusting for inflation and taxes! The investment in the S&P 500 did better by netting $117,933 in the account after removing $184,000 through quarterly distributions.

The Conservative portfolio had much lower risk and, after withdrawing the same $184,000, is left with a balance of $666,464! This is more than a 560 percent improvement in the ending capital balance when compared to the S&P 500. Why is there such a dramatic difference between the Conservative portfolio and the S&P 500 when their rates of return are not that different? The answer is that the lower volatility of the conservative portfolio prevents it from being depleted too much in down markets. The severe market declines in 1973–74 caused the S&P 500 to fall much further than the other two investments. The continued income withdrawals during such severe down periods made it very difficult for the account to rebound when the markets recovered.

Perhaps the most important message contained in this comparison is that income investors should not assume that a fixed-income investment vehicle is necessary to provide a dependable income. However, income investors must use diversified portfolios with lower variances than pure equity accounts when they seek high total rates of return. High total returns will give them the cash flow necessary to meet their retirement needs and keep pace with inflation—if they've minimized risk through diversification. Asset Class Investing has been designed to provide a prudent approach to this retirement dilemma.

INVESTOR NEED 5: DOES ASSET CLASS INVESTING PROVIDE LIQUIDITY?

Many investors have gotten hurt in the past by not thinking ahead. Often, all their investments were tied up in a single asset class, and they then had a liquidity need when that particular market segment was down, so they had to take a loss. Asset Class Investing reduces the liquidity risk. Our model portfolios are made up of equities from over 5,000 different stocks in 14 different countries. It is highly unlikely that they would all be down at the same time. When an emergency need for cash arises, usually one asset class within a portfolio is on the upswing. Dissimilar-asset-class diversification reduces overall portfolio volatility.

A prudent investor would typically maintain a cash reserve for six month's worth of expenses and for any projected, large expenditures over the next five years. These funds should be invested in short-term fixed securities with low volatility. No funds should be invested in an asset class portfolio unless they are unlikely to be needed to meet income requirements.

When an unexpected, short-term need for liquidity arises, consideration should be given to using a margin loan to obtain the funds. This will not disrupt the portfolio or cause you to change your allocation. The cost of these loans is very competitive and often can be negotiated. The maximum amount available is 50 percent of the market value of your account. A margin loan should only be used when you can pay it off within six months.

In summary, Asset Class Investing allows prudent investors to meet their needs.

Investor Need	Yes	No
Risk reduction	X	
Return enhancement	X	
Achievement of financial objectives	X	
Dependable income stream	X	
Liquidity	X	

Asset Class Investing makes traditional investments obsolete in meeting your financial needs. In the next chapter, we'll put together your asset class portfolio and get you started.

Chapter Thirteen

Putting It All Together

Y ou are now ready to build your own asset class portfolio. In this chapter, we will show you how to use each of the five key concepts and the steps necessary to construct your own investment program to meet your financial objectives. Let's get started by reviewing each of the key concepts that must be incorporated in your portfolio to prudently beat the market. Then we will compare how the introduction of each new asset class fund may effectively increase the average rate of return by over 3 percent, with less risk.

Concept 1: Utilize diversification effectively to reduce risk. If an investment could be found that would allow someone to meet their financial goals and objectives (at rates of return greater than inflation and taxes), yet let them sleep well at night, it would be the kind of investment that a prudent investor would want. In Chapters Four and Five, we learned that there was only one way to maintain a reasonable rate of return and a reasonable degree of risk at the same time. It is done through effective diversification.

We learned from Harry Markowitz, a Nobel Prize winner in economics, that there are two kinds of diversification. While nearly all diversification is good, there is effective diversification and ineffective diversification. If your investments move together, this is ineffective diversification. It's as if you hadn't diversified at all. If your investments do not move in tandem, you can accomplish effective diversification in your portfolio, because the risk in the portfolio can be less than the average risk of its components. Each of the asset class building blocks we use in this chapter utilizes this concept of risk reduction.

Concept 2: Dissimilar-price-movement diversification enhances returns. To the extent that you take advantage of effective diversification, you will increase the expected rate of return of your portfolio over time. You learned in Chapter Five that if two portfolios have the same average return, the one with the lower volatility will have the greater compound rate of return over time. In building your asset class portfolio, you can not only reduce risk but also enhance returns through effective diversification, as you will see.

Concept 3: Institutional asset class mutual funds. To build your portfolio, you need cost-effective building blocks that make use of these concepts. Institutional asset class funds are designed to meet these goals, as we discussed in Chapter Six. Similar to index fund managers, asset class mutual fund managers do not actively buy and sell securities to try and take advantage of the latest guesses of what's going to happen in the future. They recognize that markets are efficient and that the best way for them to add value to their mutual funds is to provide you with a cost-effective representation of the particular asset class you want. These asset class funds have been designed to provide you with dissimilar price movements that will allow you to diversify effectively.

Concept 4: Global Diversification. It does no good to have all your money in a single country's equity market because those investments, on average, will tend to move together. When the U.S. market periodically moves down, it tends to take most investors with it. With the introduction of international asset classes, you can provide greater protection against risk than an efficient, all-U.S. portfolio can, as well as increased expected returns, as we illustrated in Chapter Seven.

Concept 5: Design portfolios that are efficient. Your portfolio should be designed to provide you with the highest rate of return for the level of risk with which you are comfortable. In Chapter Eight, we introduced you to the math behind these concepts and determined four model asset class portfolios, which have been optimized to reach the highest expected rates of return at four different risk levels. One of these may be effective for you.

BUILDING THE ASSET CLASS PORTFOLIO, ONE STEP AT A TIME

The average investor does not utilize many of these concepts; he or she has not been exposed to them. Most investors focus on the "noise" that seems to grab the headlines—and that sets them up for failure. They think they are acting on information. In reality, there is so much noise that they cannot differentiate it from real information. They utilize active management strategies and do not stay invested for the long term. Shortly we'll compare what average investors experienced from 1976 through 1994 with what they might have experienced if they had utilized the asset class lessons in this book. First, however, we'll show the steps for building your own asset class portfolio. The first step is to decide what the allocation should be between equity and bond mutual funds.

Step 1: The 60/40 Investor

The portfolio allocation most often recommended by investment professionals has been 60 percent in the equity market and 40 percent in the bond market (see Figure 13–1).

FIGURE 13–1
Allocation: 60 Percent Equity Funds, 40 Percent Bond Funds

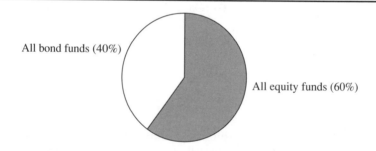

If we assume that an investor started with $100,000 in January 1976 and invested 60 percent in all equity mutual funds and 40 percent in all bond mutual funds on the *Morningstar OnDisc* database, then they would have earned the following average rate of return on their investments at the end of 1994:

Portfolio	Years	Average Compound Return%	Standard Deviation%	Growth $1
60% equity funds, 40% bond funds	19	12.02	10.89	8.65

Every dollar that investors invested in their 60%/40% allocation in 1976 would have grown to $8.65. This will be the benchmark we will use to compare the prudent methods you learned for improving your returns. This benchmark return overstates what investors would actually have earned, for three reasons:

1. First, most investors would not have been able to stay invested for that period of time without second-guessing whether they were in the best mutual fund and/or whether they should be in the stock market. They would likely have changed their allocation several times over this 19-year period, chasing performance. Many times they would have exited the market, which would have reduced their returns significantly.

2. Second, income taxes would have significantly reduced their returns. This would result from the high turnover in most retail mutual funds and the switching between funds they would have done over the years. Thus, they would have had realized capital gains, which would have been taxed.

3. Third, the average return of all equity and bond mutual funds is overstated due to "survivor bias." The average is made up of all funds that were still in existence at the end of 1994 ("survivors"). Many funds that performed poorly were either merged with more successful mutual funds or terminated.

Even though a benchmark using the average rate of return of mutual funds significantly overstates the performance of what an average investor would have realized, it does provide an effective starting point to see how Asset Class Investing can add value to your portfolio.

Step 2: The Indexed Portfolio

If you had done nothing more than use the most basic of asset class mutual funds, the S&P 500 and the Lehman Government and Corporate index, you would have achieved approximately the same returns at the same level of risk (see Figure 13–2).

All this without the high hidden cost of active management—and more free time to spend with your family. However, we have learned of many tools that you can use as building blocks that will increase your expected returns substantially without increasing risk. In the next few steps we will add asset classes without using the optimization techniques that we discussed in Chapter Eight. Even this simplistic approach adds significant value to your portfolio, as you will see.

FIGURE 13–2
Allocation: 60 Percent Equity Funds, 40 Percent Bond Funds

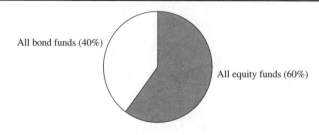

Portfolio	Years	Average Compound Return%	Standard Deviation%	Growth $1
60% equity funds, 40% bond funds	19	12.02	10.89	8.65
60% S&P 500, 40% Shearson Lehman Intermediate Gov't./Corp. Bond Index	19	12.10	10.93	8.77

Step 3: Substitute Short-Term Fixed-Income Assets

Substituting short-term fixed-income for long-term fixed-income assets significantly reduces risk while increasing expected returns. In this example, we have replaced the Shearson Lehman Intermediate Government/Corporate Bond Index which has a weighted average maturity of 3½–4½ years, with two asset classes that reduce the average maturities for the portfolio (see Figure 13–3). This lowers the risk. In addition, each new asset class has taken advantage of the matrix pricing strategy we discussed in Chapter Six, which also increases expected returns.

FIGURE 13–3
Shorten Fixed Maturities

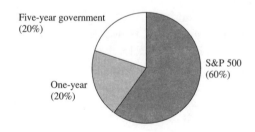

Portfolio	Years	Average Compound Return%	Standard Deviation%	Growth $1
60% equity funds, 40% bond funds	19	12.02	10.89	8.65
60% S&P 500, 40% Shearson Lehman Intermediate Gov't./Corp. Bond Index	19	12.10	10.93	8.77
Shorten fixed maturities	19	12.31	10.45	9.08

This reduction in risk (lower standard deviation) will allow you to introduce other, riskier asset classes, such as international assets.

Step 4: Utilize Global Diversification

Foreign markets and domestic markets do not move in tandem. You can add international investments that will increase the effectiveness of diversification. In this example, we divided the 60 percent allocation in equity funds between the S&P 500 index and the EAFE index (see Figure 13–4).

. **FIGURE 13–4**
Add Global Diversification

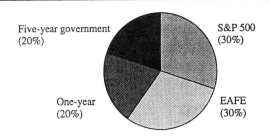

Five-year government (20%)
S&P 500 (30%)
One-year (20%)
EAFE (30%)

Portfolio	Years	Average Compound Return%	Standard Deviation%	Growth $1
60% equity funds, 40% bond funds	19	12.02	10.89	8.65
60% S&P 500, 40% Shearson Lehman Intermediate Gov't./Corp. Bond Index	19	12.10	10.93	8.77
Shorten fixed maturities	19	12.31	10.45	9.08
Add global diversification	19	13.06	9.66	10.30

Step 5: Introduce the Size Effect

The second risk factor that Eugene Fama and Kenneth French used to explain market returns was the size factor. (The first risk factor was the equity market as a whole.) They found that investors demanded to be compensated with higher returns for investing in these riskier asset classes. In this example, we have reduced the large company stock asset class by a third and reallocated that amount to small company asset classes around the world (see Figure 13–5).

FIGURE 13–5
Introduce the Size Effect

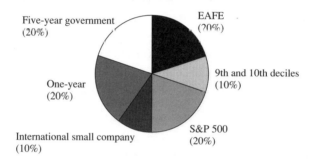

Portfolio	Years	Average Compound Return%	Standard Deviation%	Growth $1
60% equity funds, 40% bond funds	19	12.02	10.89	8.65
60% S&P 500, 40% Shearson Lehman Intermediate Gov't./Corp. Bond Index	19	12.10	10.93	8.77
Shorten fixed maturities	19	12.31	10.45	9.08
Add global diversification	19	13.06	9.66	10.30
Introduce the size effect	19	14.24	8.68	12.55

It is interesting to note that the introduction of this risky asset class reduces the portfolio risk while increasing returns.

Step 6: Introduce the High Book-to-Market Effect

The third risk factor that Fama and French used to explain market returns was the relative book-to-market ratio (BTM). They found that this risk factor was rewarded most significantly outside the United States. The replacement of the S&P 500 index and EAFE index with a high-BTM asset class increases returns significantly while reducing risk (see Figure 13–6).

FIGURE 13–6
Utilize the High-BTM Risk Factor

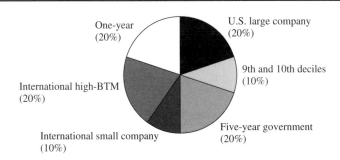

One-year
(20%)

U.S. large company
(20%)

9th and 10th deciles
(10%)

International high-BTM
(20%)

Five-year government
(20%)

International small company
(10%)

Portfolio	Years	Average Compound Return%	Standard Deviation%	Growth $1
60% equity funds, 40% bond funds	19	12.02	10.89	8.65
60% S&P 500, 40% Shearson Lehman Intermediate Gov't./Corp. Bond Index	19	12.10	10.93	8.77
Shorten fixed maturities	19	12.31	10.45	9.08
Add global diversification	19	13.06	9.66	10.30
Introduce the size effect	19	14.24	8.68	12.55
Utilize the high-BTM risk factor	19	15.68	9.78	15.93

Implementing Asset Class Investing allows prudent investors to beat the market returns significantly. Using our benchmark average investor portfolio, we were able to increase the growth of $1 over the 19 years from $8.65 to $15.93. This represents a more than 75 percent increase in the ending value of the portfolio over our benchmark. Most investors did not typically make returns anywhere near this benchmark.

GETTING A QUICK START ON YOUR OWN ASSET CLASS PORTFOLIO

Step 1: Identify your investment fund. How much money can you leave untouched for five years in an investment portfolio—money you won't need for emergencies or income? This is the dollar amount you should start with.

Step 2: Decide the risk you are willing to take. In the Appendix, we have illustrated each of the four model portfolios we built in Chapter Eight. Examine the negative-return years. Most investors are not concerned with standard deviations, but with the absolute loss of capital. The worst financial recession since World War II was during 1973–74. Look to see which portfolios would have been able to weather the storm, knowing that the five-year periods were all positive. No one can predict that the next two years will not be as bad as 1973–74. You should decide on what risk you are willing to take, based on the assumption that the next two years will be the same as 1973–74.

Step 3: Consider using one of our model portfolios. Choose one that most closely aligns with the amount of risk you are willing to take.

Step 4: Select the most appropriate asset class mutual funds. Choose the ones that best incorporate, on a cost-effective basis, the concepts we have discussed. In Chapter Six, we list many of the currently available retail asset class funds.

Step 5: Open an account at one of the discount brokerage firms. It is unlikely that one mutual fund family will have all the asset class mutual funds you will need for your portfolio. Custodians, such as discount brokers, will make the rebalancing task much easier to complete.

Step 6: Rebalance at least annually. The optimization strategies that we discussed in Chapter Nine are difficult for individual investors to accomplish. However, by systematically rebalancing to the original model portfolio at least annually, you will gradually sell those asset classes that have gone up, while buying those that currently have lower returns. This approach eliminates the negative results of being driven by emotions.

MORE PROOF THAT ASSET CLASS INVESTING WORKS: RELATIVE PERFORMANCE OF THE MODEL PORTFOLIOS

Let's compare how the four model portfolios we discussed in Chapter Eight, enhanced with the techniques of Chapters Nine and Ten, would have performed relative to all balanced retail mutual funds that have been in existence since 1975 (see Table 13–1). It is easy to see how Asset Class Investing can help you prudently beat the market.

TABLE 13–1
Asset Class versus Balanced Retail Funds

Fund Name	15-Year Annualized Return	15-Year Standard Deviation
Aggressive	17.72%	13.13%
Moderate	16.69	10.43
Fidelity Puritan	15.45	10.49
Conservative	15.42	8.03
CGM Mutual	14.72	15.09
Phoenix Income and Growth/A	14.52	9.95
State Farm Balanced	14.08	12.20
Delaware/A	14.01	15.58
Vanguard/Wellington	13.67	11.41
Dodge and Cox Balanced	13.51	11.07
MFS Total Return/A	13.50	10.92
United Continental Income	13.42	12.32
Defensive	13.38	5.77
IDS Mutual	13.15	10.33
United Retirement Shares	13.12	12.22
Kemper Total Return/A	13.08	14.87
George Putnam of Boston/	12.87	11.74
American Balanced	12.80	10.10
Sentinel Balanced	12.54	10.17
Fonders Balanced	12.42	9.53
T. Rowe Price Balanced	12.39	11.28
New England Balanced/A	12.09	14.91
EV Traditional Investors	12.04	10.48
Alliance Balanced Shares/A	11.68	11.57
Stock and Bond/A	11.66	8.42
Keystone Custodian K-1	11.56	10.65
Pax World	11.17	11.33
Composite Bond and Stock/A	11.07	10.60

It is very hard to stay on track with the tremendous amount of noise present. Often, things are not as they appear. For many investors, having a qualified investment advisor who can help them stay on track will add substantial value. Other investors may wish to travel this road alone. In the next chapter, we will examine the pros and cons of having an investment advisor—and, if you chose to have one, how to find one.

Chapter Fourteen

Selecting a Money Management Firm and Financial Advisor

I n this chapter we will uncover why many investors feel uncomfortable working with investment professionals, how to evaluate whether it is cost effective for you to utilize a financial advisor, and, if so, how you select your investment advisory team.

WHY DO MANY INVESTORS FEEL UNCOMFORTABLE WORKING WITH INVESTMENT PROFESSIONALS?

Our firm recently asked investors about their concerns in meeting their financial needs. Four major concerns were shared. Asset Class Investing can overcome all four.

1. First, many investors felt uncomfortable dealing with the financial service industry, due to the transactional nature of the compensation. In the past, unless your investment assets exceeded $1 million, it was very difficult to hire a competent, fee-based money manager. For that reason, most individual investors were forced to work with insurance agents or financial planners who were paid on a commission basis by investment product sponsors. Many investors felt that the recommendations they received from these sources were suspect due to the conflict of interest inherent in the commission.

Utilizing Asset Class Investing allows investors to pay a predetermined fee to an independent financial advisor, not a commission. The fee is paid as you go. The advisor has to perform to keep your account. If you terminate the relationship, the fees are prorated. If you close your account one day after you open it, you will be billed ⅟₃₆₅th of your annual fee. Contrast that with a traditional financial advisor, who earns his compensation up front on the initial transaction.

2. The second strongest investor concern was that they were unsure of how they were doing. The limited performance reporting on the monthly brokerage statements was difficult to understand. Tracking performance was particularly troublesome if the investor was working with more than one brokerage account. It was also difficult to track the underlying investments. Without accurate, well-defined performance measures, it's impossible to decide what actions should be taken. In addition, individual investors must keep track of their cost basis for tax purposes. Financial advisors also keep track of this tax information and will ensure that each sale is done on a tax-effective basis. A financial advisor will provide you with the timely information you need to better understand your portfolio's performance.

3. The third most common problem was that there was so much noise, investors did not feel comfortable taking any action. Investors need an effective filter to determine what is information, regardless of whether they subscribe to such publications as *Money, Forbes, Fortune, Business Week,* or *The Wall Street Journal.* Frequently, these periodicals contain conflicting recommendations, although they draw from the same data. In today's information age, one challenge is dealing with information effectively and using it to your advantage. Financial advisors can bring their years of financial expertise to use information to your advantage.

4. The fourth concern the investors expressed was the fear that decisions would be made for emotional reasons rather than as part of a well-defined, academically sound approach. Financial advisors who utilize Asset Class Investing create a disciplined investment approach.

WHEN IS IT COST EFFECTIVE TO WORK WITH A FINANCIAL ADVISOR?

There are two advantages to having a financial advisor help you put your asset class investment program together. The first is it spares you the time that's consumed when you have sole responsibility for drafting your investment policy statement, implementing it, and reviewing your portfolio on a quarterly basis. Most investors don't have the time to put this together and find it more cost effective to hire a professional to assume these responsibilities.

The second reason for using a financial advisor is that advisors often have access to institutional asset class mutual funds that are not available to the public. These institutional asset class mutual funds typically have significantly lower costs, tax advantages, and higher expected returns than retail mutual funds. This combination of savings and return enhancement will often be greater than the financial advisor's fee. The fees that advisors charge typically range from 2.0 percent to 0.4 percent of your investment, depending on the size of the account. Unfortunately, many advisors have account balance minimums of $50,000 or more, which means you may have to go it alone if you cannot meet the minimum.

HOW TO SELECT YOUR INVESTMENT ADVISORY TEAM

An investment advisory team normally consists of two members: the financial advisor and the money management firm. The financial advisor is usually an independent investment advisor whose only motive should be to represent his clients' interests. He will work with you to write your investment policy statement and maintain it on a quarterly basis. To implement asset class strategies, the financial advisor will identify a money management firm that is capable of managing your portfolio of institutional asset class mutual funds. Let's look first at the money management firm.

The Crucial Qualifications You Should Seek in Your Money Management Firm

There are five qualifications you should look for in a money management firm.[1]

1. Independence. The money management firm should not be engaged in, affiliated with, or controlled by any organization in the brokerage, insurance, underwriting, or other financial field. It should not be owned or organized in any way that could jeopardize its ability to render independent advice in the clients' best interests.

2. Philosophy. The firm should have a consistent philosophy that does not confuse investing with trading or speculating. And it should have a proven, effective record—in bad as well as in good years, under all types of economic and political conditions—indicating that it has the discipline to follow its philosophy.

3. Specialization. The firm should not be a financial department store. Its efforts should be confined to investment analysis and portfolio management, rather than spread out over a whole range of other, thinly related activities.

4. Teamwork. A competent and experienced staff that works together closely is more likely to produce effective results than either the superstar system or a big, loosely knit organization whose internal communications are cumbersome and often inconsistent.

5. Responsibility. This is a tough one to assess. But anyone who manages other people's money must regard it as a serious trust and not as a "money game" or an exercise in mathematical equations.

You should only work with a money management firm that can meet these five qualifications, consistent with your new understanding of how investment markets work. The way to find a money manager is through a financial advisor—but not just any financial advisor.

How to Select Your Financial Advisor

Many financial advisors are ill-equipped to assist you with Asset Class Investing. These include insurance salespeople and tax advisors who may have changed their titles to "financial planner" to gain a marketing advantage. Often, these individuals want to sell you a product, not assist you. The difference between working with a good and an average financial advisor will have a significant impact on your success. Let's look at one study completed by Dalbar Financial Services Inc. to see how big this difference can be.

This study, reflected in Table 14-1, shows how individual investors did on their own and with financial advisors. We have also included for comparison the model portfolios' performances for the same time period, so you can see the significant difference in returns realized by working with a qualified financial advisor.

The study measured the total returns earned by investors who purchased directly marketed investment products, versus the returns earned by those who used the services of a financial advisor over a 10-year period. While using a financial advisor did improve overall returns versus do-it-yourself investing, it added value in only one dimension.

From January 1984 through September 1993, equity investors using financial advisors realized total returns of 90.21 percent versus a total return of 70.23 percent for the do-it-yourself investors. The study concluded that individuals who go it alone are more likely to try to time markets rather than hold assets for the long term. If you used the services of a financial advisor, you would have increased your returns on average by 20 percent over time. That's a pretty good case for working with any advisor.

Let's take it a step further. During the same time period, the model asset class portfolios substantially outperformed investors both working with advisors and on their own (see Table 14-1).

TABLE 14–1

	Total Return 1/84–9/93 %
Dalbar Results	
Investors on their own	70.23%
Investors with advisors	90.21
Model Portfolio	
Defensive	258.98
Conservative	374.44
Moderate	462.99
Aggressive	549.07

The Dalbar study confirms what we have suspected: On average, individuals managing their own money lack the training necessary to reach their financial goals. Those working with an average financial advisor did a little better. As we have learned, most financial advisors will attempt to add value by trying to pick securities, stocks, or mutual funds—or worse, tell you which way the market's going by way of market timing. They follow traditional investment strategies—strategies that all academic studies conclude don't work. Most financial advisors simply do not understand the concepts featured in this book, or choose to ignore them. It is critical to find a specialist who understands Asset Class Investing and utilizes the latest tools and research, previously available to only the largest pension plans, to ensure that you reach your financial goals. Let's look at how to find a financial advisor and what questions to ask.

Traditionally, financial advisors are found by referrals from other satisfied investors, a friend, a certified public accountant (CPA), or an attorney. Unfortunately, this method has two major pitfalls. One, in today's litigious society, people are less willing to refer you to anyone due to the implied endorsement. Second, many CPAs, attorneys, and individual investors don't understand the concepts presented in this book.

THE CRUCIAL QUALIFICATIONS YOU SHOULD EXPECT FROM YOUR FINANCIAL ADVISOR

- Financial advisors must construct portfolios according to Modern Portfolio Theory. They should understand and agree that market timing and individual stock selection are unreliable investment management techniques and should not follow those strategies. Modern Portfolio Theory offers the most academically sound approach to investing, as attested to by the Nobel Prize in Economics awarded to Harry Markowitz for originating this practical theory.

- The advisor should be compensated on a fee-only basis rather than by brokerage commissions. Advisors who work on commission may be more likely to recommend more frequent transactions in your portfolio.

- A fee-only advisor has a more objective position toward his or her clients and is more likely to follow one of the modern investment strategies.

- Determine your own time horizon for investing and communicate that time frame to your advisor. No one should ever invest in equities unless they have at least a five-year time horizon. Even if you are retired, a five-year or longer time horizon fits most situations.

- One year out of every four, the stock market goes down; no one has ever been able to predict accurately which year that will be. For that reason, your portfolio should be designed with a five-year time horizon, keeping in mind that when that one down year happens, you can weather the storm. An advisor can help you determine your level of risk in down years. Don't set yourself up for failure. Recognize that there are going to be down years, and put yourself in a position to ride through those years—or don't get in the equity market.

- The advisor should work with you to set target rates of return—the returns you will need on your entire investment portfolio to achieve your objectives. A fee-only advisor can show you different models and mixes of investments that have the highest probability of achieving your goals.

- The advisor should write an investment policy statement. This statement should provide specific instructions to an investment counselor and cover such topics as: target rates of return, risk tolerance, anticipated withdrawals or contributions, regulatory issues, and desired holding periods of asset classes. One of the best examples would be to look at how your portfolio would have performed during the 1973–74 recessionary period.

- The advisor should purchase selected asset classes with institutional asset class mutual funds, if available. To minimize risk, a portfolio should be put together with asset classes that have a low correlation, which means when one class of assets is down, another in the same portfolio is likely to be up.

- The advisor should rebalance your portfolio periodically. If an asset differs by more than 5 percent from its original target allocation, then either buy more or sell some of the assets until the target percentage is restored. Reoptimization on a quarterly basis will add the most value, if used effectively.

- Measure your investment performance quarterly. The advisor should provide some method of measurement and determine whether the market value of your portfolio is growing fast enough to achieve your target objective by using time-weighted rates of return.

Often, investors and inexperienced advisors believe that once they build an asset class portfolio, they won't need to make any changes. If we look back only five years, we can see that Asset Class Investing has improved dramatically. Over the next five years, it is likely that we will see even greater changes. It would be foolish for any investor not to take advantage of this knowledge. Finding an advisor to help you implement this strategy and keep you abreast of any new improvements will add tremendous value to your portfolio.

We wish you the best of success in "beating the market." You have prudently earned it!

We wish you the best of success in "beating the market." You have prudently earned it!

ENDNOTES

[1]Babson, D., "The Commercial and Financial Chronicle" (June 28, 1973), pp. 12–13; excerpted in C. Ellis, *Classics II: Another Investor's Anthology* (Business One Irwin, 1991), pp. 550–51

Appendix

Formulas

CASH AND EQUIVALENTS

The first asset class we've chosen is cash and equivalents. Most investors will use a money market fund as part of their fixed-income asset class. In research completed by Eugene Fama, the best indicator of future interest rates is today's interest rates. The expected rate of return for a money market fund is very simple to calculate: It is the current yield of that money market instrument. The formula for our money market fund estimate would be:

$$R_{mm} = t_{90}$$

where

R_{mm} = Money market expected return

t_{90} = Observed 90-day Treasury bill return

ONE-YEAR HIGH-QUALITY CORPORATE

The second fixed-income asset class is a one-year fixed-income portfolio. This portfolio's expected rate of return will not be just the one-year maturity if you utilize a matrix pricing strategy. This strategy, as outlined in Chapter Six, is able to capture a trading premium over and above the 90-day Treasury bill, which is its benchmark.

The expected rate of return is:

$$R_f = t_{90} + P_t$$

where

R_f = One-year fixed-income expected return

t_{90} =   Observed 90-day Treasury bill return

P_t =   Observed premium of one-year
                                fixed-income strategy over 90-day
                                Treasury bill return

FIVE-YEAR U.S. GOVERNMENT

The five-year U.S. government institutional asset class portfolio utilizes
the matrix pricing strategy illustrated in Chapter Six. The expected rate of
return is:

R_g = $t_{90} + P_t$

where

R_g =   Five-year U.S. government bonds' expected return

t_{90} =   Observed 90-day Treasury bill return

P_t =   Observed premium of five-year U.S.
                                government strategy over 90-day
                                Treasury bill return

U.S. LARGE COMPANY STOCKS

In calculating the expected rate of return for the U.S. large company stock
asset class, we've utilized the S&P 500 index as our benchmark. The
expected rate of return for the five-year period is based on the risk-free
investment plus the risk premium associated with market risk. Investors
are rewarded for taking this market risk. This risk premium can be estimated historically by determining the excess returns the S&P 500 index
earned over five-year government bonds. Investors with a five-year time
horizon would have, as their risk-free investments, five-year government
bonds. To be enticed to take the additional market risk of the S&P 500, a
compensating premium would have to be earned.

To determine today's expected return on the S&P 500 index, you simply observe the current yield to maturity for five-year government bonds
and add the market risk premium. To calculate this premium, you subtract the arithmetic average return of the S&P 500 for the longest period

available, 1926 through 1994, less the arithmetic average return for the five-year government bond.

The expected rate of return is:

R_{us}	$=$	$t_{5yr} + P_e$
where		
R_{us}	$=$	U.S. large company stocks' expected return
t_{5yr}	$=$	Observed five-year zero coupon Treasury bond return
P_e	$=$	Observed premium of S&P 500 index over five-year zero coupon Treasury bond

U.S. SMALL COMPANY STOCKS

With small company stocks, we have an additional risk premium for which we're rewarded over the U.S. large company stocks. It's very logical if you stop and realize that no one in their right mind would buy small companies if they had the same returns as large companies. Small companies are subject to downturns in times of recession and often go out of business. The risk is substantially higher. You need to be rewarded for the extra risk.

To calculate this risk premium, you subtract the arithmetic average return of the U.S. small company stocks for the longest period available, 1926 through 1994, less the arithmetic average return of the S&P 500. To determine today's expected returns for U.S. small company stocks, you simply observe the current yield to maturity for five-year government bonds, add the market risk premium, and add the small company stock premium. The expected rate of return is:

R_{sc}	$=$	$t_{5yr} + P_e + P_{sc}$
where		
R_{sc}	$=$	U.S. large company stocks' expected return
t_{5yr}	$=$	Observed five-year zero coupon Treasury bond return
P_e	$=$	Observed premium of S&P 500 index over five-year zero coupon Treasury bond

P_{sc} = Observed arithmetic small company (9th and 10th decile) returns over the S&P 500 index premium

INTERNATIONAL LARGE COMPANY STOCKS

Investors demand a return for the risk they take. In calculating the expected rates of return, we want to utilize as long a time series of information as possible. Unfortunately, in the international markets, the time series of information available is much less than for the U.S. market. This century saw some major events that changed things dramatically internationally: World War I, World War II, etc. For our benchmark indexes, we have used Morgan Stanley's EAFE.

To calculate the expected rate of return, we use a relative equity premium, the observed equity premium of the S&P 500 index multiplied by the international large company stocks' relative risk as contrasted with the S&P 500 index. To determine today's expected return for international large company stocks, you observe the current yield to maturity for five-year government bonds and add the market risk premium adjusted for relative risk. The expected rate of return is:

$$R_{il} = t_{5yr} + \left(\frac{\sigma_{il}}{\sigma_{us}}\right)(P_e)$$

where

R_{il} = International large company stocks' expected return

t_{5yr} = Observed five-year zero coupon Treasury bond return

σ_{il} = Standard deviation of international large company stocks

σ_{us} = Standard deviation of S&P 500 index

P_e = Observed premium of S&P 500 index over five-year zero coupon Treasury bond

INTERNATIONAL SMALL COMPANY STOCKS

The international small company stocks are calculated in the same manner as the international large company stocks.

$$R_{is} \quad = \quad t_{5yr} + \left(\frac{\sigma_{is}}{\sigma_{us}}\right)(P_e)$$

where

R_{is}	=	International small company stock's expected return
t_{5yr}	=	Observed five-year zero coupon Treasury bond return
σ_{is}	=	Standard deviation of international small company stocks
σ_{us}	=	Standard deviation of S&P 500 index
P_e	=	Observed premium of S&P 500 index over five-year zero coupon Treasury bond

STANDARD DEVIATION

Let's examine the risk of each portfolio by calculating the standard deviation. The formula for standard deviation is:

$$\sigma \quad = \quad \frac{\sqrt{(X_1 - \overline{X})^2 + (X_2 - \overline{X})^2 + \ldots + (X_N - \overline{X})^2}}{N}$$

Standard deviation = Square root of variance

$$\text{Variance} \quad = \quad \frac{(X_1 - \overline{X})^2 + (X_2 - \overline{X})^2 + \ldots + (X_N - \overline{X})^2}{N}$$

where:

$\overline{X}$	=	Average value of the variable for the period observed
N	=	Number of observations[1]

To determine the standard deviation for each of the asset classes, we have used their historical standard deviations. In any statistical measure, we want to use as much information as is available for as long a time period as possible, unless we have some valid reasons for discarding time series information. Many publications tend to use relatively short periods

---

[1] Purists will divide by N-1 instead of N to ensure that the estimate of variance is an unbiased estimate of the true or underlying variance.

in calculating the standard deviation, such as 3, 5, 10, or even 15 years. These relatively short periods of time don't allow us to really understand the true risk components. For example, over the last 10 years, bonds have had the best returns ever. The '80s was a decade during which it was almost impossible for the stock market not to look good. During 1973 and 1974, however, we had our worst financial recession since World War II, but most studies ignore this period.

CORRELATION COEFFICIENT

The formula to determine the correlation coefficients between two asset classes is the covariance between X and Y = average of $(X - \bar{X})(Y - \bar{Y})$.

$$\text{Correlation coefficient} \quad = \quad \frac{(X_1 - \bar{X})^2 + (X_2 - \bar{X})}{(\sigma_x)(\sigma_y)}$$

Our portfolio's expected rate of return is simply the average weighted expected return for each of the asset classes. The risk for a portfolio is determined by calculating its standard deviation. Due to the asset classes not moving in tandem, the standard deviation is not the weighted average, but the portfolio's variance.

Portfolio variance $\quad = \quad w_1^2 s_1^2 + 2w_1 w_2 r_{12} s_1 s_2 + w_2^2 s_2^2$

where

w_1, w_2 $\quad = \quad$ Proportions of the portfolio invested in assets 1 and 2

s_1, s_2 $\quad = \quad$ Standard deviations of returns of assets 1 and 2

r_{12} $\quad = \quad$ Correlations between returns of assets 1 and 2

In the next section, this risk factor is determined by using William Sharpe's Capital Asset Pricing Model (CAPM).

SINGLE-FACTOR MODEL (CAPM)

$R(t) - RF(t)$ $\quad = \quad$ $\alpha + \beta[RM(t) - RF(t)] + e(t)$

Average expected return - Treasury bill = Average excess return + β [Market return] - Treasury bill

This model explains 70 percent of the variability of returns.

THREE-FACTOR MODEL

$$R(t) - RF(t) = \alpha + \beta \, [RM(t) - RF(t)] + sSMB(t) + hHML(t) + e(t)$$

Average expected return - Treasury bill = Average excess return + β [Market return] - Treasury bill + Sensitivity to size [Small stocks - Large stocks] + Sensitivity to BTM [High-BTM–Low-BTM]

This model explains 95 percent of the variability of returns.

TABLE A-1
Model Portfolio Performance

1 Year Ending	Inflation	T-Bills	T-Bonds	S & P 500	Small Co. Stocks	EAFE	Defensive	Conservative	Moderate	Aggressive
	%	%	%	%	%	%	%	%	%	%
12/31/72	3.41	3.82	5.68	18.97	-0.27	37.65	8.68	15.23	20.52	26.01
12/31/73	8.77	6.93	-1.10	-14.67	-38.96	-14.17	3.34	-2.51	-7.19	-11.39
12/31/74	12.20	8.00	4.34	-26.46	-28.64	-22.13	1.43	-7.37	-14.18	-19.71
12/31/75	7.02	5.81	9.18	37.23	65.71	37.04	18.27	29.89	39.55	46.93
12/31/76	4.82	5.07	16.77	23.85	51.06	3.79	15.31	18.42	21.27	23.35
12/31/77	6.76	5.13	-0.65	-7.18	26.81	19.37	5.83	12.75	18.73	26.50
12/31/78	9.03	7.21	-1.19	6.58	25.80	34.33	9.76	16.93	22.70	29.37
12/31/79	13.33	10.39	-1.21	18.42	43.18	6.16	12.13	13.04	14.24	14.48
12/31/80	12.40	11.25	-3.96	32.40	41.84	24.45	11.93	16.00	19.89	23.74
12/31/81	8.94	14.72	1.86	-4.91	-2.69	-1.04	18.73	15.03	11.59	7.80
12/31/82	3.86	10.53	40.37	21.40	28.01	-0.83	22.49	19.19	15.86	13.98
12/31/83	3.80	8.80	0.69	22.52	39.66	24.55	13.24	19.25	24.47	28.55
12/31/84	4.01	9.79	15.54	6.26	-6.67	7.88	10.57	9.84	9.31	8.40
12/31/85	3.76	7.72	30.94	32.17	24.66	56.73	23.57	31.11	35.37	40.54
12/31/86	1.14	6.16	24.45	18.46	6.85	69.98	19.20	26.26	30.10	33.87
12/31/87	4.43	5.48	-2.71	5.23	-9.30	24.93	7.57	12.46	15.92	20.71
12/31/88	4.42	6.35	9.67	16.81	22.88	28.60	11.92	17.32	21.59	24.52
12/31/89	4.65	8.37	18.11	31.49	10.19	10.78	13.71	17.20	19.94	21.92
12/31/90	6.09	7.81	6.19	-3.17	-21.56	-23.20	3.78	-2.93	-8.44	-12.63
12/31/91	3.06	5.60	19.26	30.12	44.63	12.47	14.45	16.57	18.12	19.13
12/31/92	3.02	3.49	9.41	7.31	23.34	-11.81	7.28	6.42	5.85	3.95
12/31/93	2.75	2.89	18.24	9.60	20.97	32.87	12.64	18.98	23.21	26.07
12/31/94	2.69	3.90	-7.77	1.28	3.11	8.01	-0.01	2.07	4.14	6.20
Max	13.33	14.72	40.37	37.23	65.71	69.98	23.57	31.11	39.55	46.93
Average	5.84	7.18	9.22	12.34	16.11	15.93	11.56	13.96	15.76	17.49
Min	1.14	2.89	-7.77	-26.46	-38.96	-23.20	-0.01	-7.37	-14.18	-19.71
STD	3.41	2.85	12.12	16.49	26.56	23.51	6.38	9.71	13.10	16.44

Material Sources:

Inflation: Courtesy or Roger G. Ibbotson and Rex A. Sinquefield, Stocks,
                                    Bonds, Bills and Inflation: The Past and the Future, Dow Jones,
                                    1989. Ibbotson Associates, Chicago, annual updates work by
                                    Roger G. Ibbotson and Rex A. Sinquefield. Used with permission.
                                    All rights reserved.

Thirty-Day Treasury Bills: Source: as above.

Long-Term Treasury Bonds: Average maturity: 20 years. Source: as above.

S&P 500 Index: Source: as above.

EAFE Index: Courtesy of Morgan Stanley & Company. Europe, Australia, and
                                    Far East Index.

   January 1972 - Present: EAFE Index including gross dividend ($).

Small Co. Stocks:

   January 1972 - December 1972:   CRSP Database, NYSE & AMEX, rebalanced quarterly
   January 1973 - December 1981:   CRSP Database, NYSE & AMEX & OTC, rebalanced quarterly
   January 1982 - Present: U.S. 9-10 Small Company Portfolio net of all fees/Small
                                    Company Subtrust net of administrative fees only.

THE FOLLOWING ASSET CLASSES, ALONG WITH SMALL CO. STOCKS, ABOVE, WERE
USED TO CONSTRUCT THE MODEL PORTFOLIOS:

U.S. Large Cap Value Portfolio:

   January 1972 - March 1993:   Fama-French Large Cap Value Strategy, Simulates Dimensional's
                                    hold range and estimated trading costs. Courtesy of Fama-French
                                    and CRSP: Deciles 1-5 Size, (.7) BTM
   April 1993 - Present: U.S. Large Cap Value Portfolio net of all fees.

DFA International High Book to Market Portfolio:

   January 1975 - March 1993:   International High BTM (Value) Value-weighted Unhedged $
                                    (Top 30% BTM). Simulated DFA Strategy (Maximum Japan
                                    38%), Courtesy of Fama-French & MSCI. Includes Japan, U.K.,
                                    France, Germany, Switzerland, Netherlands, Hong Kong,
                                    Australia, Italy, Belgium, Spain (rebalanced quarterly).
   April 1993 - June 1993:   EAFE Index (MSCI) Substituted temporarily.
   July 1993 - Present: DFA International High Book to Market Portfolio net of all fees.
                                    Countries include all of the above and Sweden as of October 1994.

United Kingdom Small Company Portfolio:

   January 1972 - March 1986:   Hoare Govett Smaller Companies Index, London School of
                                    Business.
   April 1986 - Present: Dimensional's U.K. Small Company Portfolio net of all fees.

Continental Small Company Portfolio:

   July 1988 - Present: Dimensional's Continental Small Company Portfolio net of all fees.
                                    Countries included: Belgium, France, Germany, Italy, Netherlands,
                                    Spain, Switzerland, Include Sweden as of October 1994.

Japanese Small Company Portfolio:

   January 1972 - March 1986:   Japanese Small Companies. Smaller half of first section, Tokyo
                                    Stock Exchange. The Nomura Securities Investment Trust
                                    Management Co., Ltd., Tokyo - rebalanced semi-annually.
   April 1986 - Present: Japanese Small Company portfolio net of all fees.

DFA One-Year Fixed Income Portfolio:

   January - 1972 - July 1983:   Simulation using CD returns.
   August 1983 - Present: DFA One-Year Fixed Income Portfolio net of all fees

DFA Five-Year Government Fixed Income Portfolio:

   January 1972 - May 1987:   Simulation using U.S. Government instruments.
   June 1987 - Present: DFA Five-Year Government Fixed Income Portfolio net of all fees.

SUBJECT INDEX

A

Active money management, 12, 29, 33, 38, 93, 94
Allocating your portfolio, 98-99
  calculate correlation coefficients of asset classes, 98
  determine expected rate of return, 98
  identify risk tolerance, 99
  know risk of asset class, 98
  solve for optimal combination, 99
American Economic Review, 28
AMEX, 111
Arnott, Robert D., 63
Asset class, 2-3
  allocating your portfolio among, 98-99
  dissimilar-price-movement, 54
  fixed-income, 72, 74, 78; *see also* Bonds
    and inflation, 72
    performance versus equities, 72-73
    and portfolio risk level, 73, 76
    risks of investing in, 79-80
  international; *see* Global diversification
  and low correlation, 43
  and negative covariance, 43
  study of individual, 29-30
  and volatility, 73
  as whole market segments, 50, 58
Asset Class Investing, 2-5; *see also* Investment strategies
  and equities, 57
  fundamental ingredients in, 43
  and investor needs, 133-139
    dependable income stream produced, 136-138
    financial goals reached, 135-136
    liquidity provided, 138-139
    return increase, 134-135
    risk reduction, 133-134
  key concepts of 140-150; *see also* Dissimilar price movements; Effective diversification;

Asset Class Investing—*Cont.*
  key concepts of—*Cont.*
    Efficient portfolio design; Global diversification; Institutional asset class mutual funds; Key concepts
  and the long-term investor, 47
  versus other investment methodologies, 50, 51, 54
  philosophy of, 53-54
  and risk reduction, 48
  and volatility reduction, 48, 49
Asset class portfolio
  building, 141-147
    global diversification, 145
    high book-to-market effect, 147
    indexed portfolio, 143
    60/40 investor, 142-143
    size effect, 146
    short-term fixed-income funds, 144-145
  quick start, 148
    consider model portfolio, 148
    decide level of risk, 148
    identify investment fund, 148
    open discount brokerage account, 148
    rebalance annually, 148
    select appropriate funds, 148
    relative performance, 149-150
Assets, 5, 40, 41, 42, 45

B

Bachelier, Louis, 25
Bear market, 52
Behavior of Stock Prices, The (Fama), 27
Bogle, John, 37
Bonds, 73, 74, 75-76, 88
Book-to-market risk, 108-110
Bowen, John, 1
Brokerage firms, 6
BTM; *see* Book-to-market risk

167

Thank you for choosing Irwin Professional Publishing (formerly Business One Irwin) for your information needs. If you are part of a corporation, professional association, or government agency, consider our newest option: Custom Publishing. This service helps you create customized books, manuals, and other materials from your organization's resources, select chapters of our books, or both.

Irwin Professional Publishing books are also excellent resources for training/educational programs, premiums, and incentives. For information on volume discounts or custom publishing, call 1-800-634-3966.